Marriage As Gift
A CATHOLIC APPROACH

Josephine Robinson

Pauline
BOOKS & MEDIA
Boston

Library of Congress Cataloging-in-Publication Data
Robinson, Josephine.
  Marriage as gift : a Catholic approach / Josephine Robinson. — 1st North American ed.
      p. cm.
  Originally pub.: Marriage and gift. London : St. Pauls, 2004.
  Includes bibliographical references.
  ISBN 0-8198-4858-1 (pbk.)
  1. Marriage—Religious aspects—Catholic Church. I. Robinson, Josephine. Marriage and gift. II. Title.
  BX2250.R635 2007
  248.4'82—dc22

                                    2006038140

Cover design by Rosana Usselmann

Cover photo by Tetra Images

Original edition published in English under the title: *Marriage and Gift*

Copyright © ST PAULS UK 2004

First North American Edition, 2007

Published by Pauline Books & Media, 50 Saint Paul's Avenue, Boston, MA 02130-3491. www.pauline.org.

Printed in the U.S.A.

Pauline Books & Media is the publishing house of the Daughters of St. Paul, an international congregation of women religious serving the Church with the communications media.

1 2 3 4 5 6 7 8 9   12 11 10 09 08 07

Contents

Acknowledgments . . . . *v*

Introduction *1*

CHAPTER 1
Before Marriage *2*

CHAPTER 2
Preparing for Marriage *17*

CHAPTER 3
Love and Marriage: The Body in God's Plan *40*

CHAPTER 4
Male and Female. *61*

CHAPTER 5
Openness to Life. *81*

CHAPTER 6
New Life, New Excitement *101*

CHAPTER 7
The Domestic Church. *117*

CHAPTER 8
Difficulties *133*

CHAPTER 9
Married Saints and Their Witness *151*

CHAPTER 10
A Backward Look at Marriage and Its Meaning *173*

Afterword *186*

Appendix *187*

Notes *191*

Acknowledgments

Many people have assisted me in writing this book. First of all, I would like to thank Annabel Robson, of St. Paul's Publishing (Pauline Books & Media in the U.S.A.), who has given me much help and continual support. I also wish to express my thanks to Canon Michael Brockie, Fr. Christopher Basden, Fr. Hilary Crewe, and Fr. Alexander Sherbrooke, who have all given me their time and provided many insights. Finally, I would like to mention my friends in the Association of Catholic Women with whom I have teased out many of these ideas and whose help has been invaluable.

Prayer for the Family

by Pope John Paul II

Lord God, from you every family
in heaven and on earth takes its name.
Father, you are Love and Life.
Through your Son, Jesus Christ, born of woman,
and through the Holy Spirit, fountain of divine charity,
grant that every family on earth may become
for each successive generation
a true shrine of life and love.
Grant that your grace may guide the thoughts and actions
of husbands and wives

for the good of their families and of all the families
in the world.
Grant that the young may find in the family
solid support for their human dignity
and for their growth in truth and love.
Grant that love,
strengthened by the grace of the sacrament of Marriage,
may prove mightier than all the weakness and trials
through which our families sometimes pass.
Through the intercession of the Holy Family of Nazareth,
grant that the Church may fruitfully carry out
her worldwide mission in the family and through the family.
Through Christ our Lord,
who is the Way, the Truth, and the Life,
for ever and ever. Amen.

VOICES, VOL. XVIII: No. 1
LENT-EASTER, 2003

Introduction

All tragedies are finish'd by a death
All comedies are ended with a marriage.

(BYRON, *DON JUAN,* CANTO III ST. 9)

Dante called his great poem of Christian aspiration *The Divine Comedy.* In the Bible, in only the second chapter of that vast work, we read that "a man leaves his father and his mother and clings to his wife, and they become one flesh."[1] Not only is marriage spoken of in the first book of the Old Testament, but it appears in the very last chapter of the New Testament as well. In the Book of Revelation, attributed to St. John the Evangelist, we are told of the "wife of the Lamb"—the Lamb of God, whose bride is the New Jerusalem, the Holy City, the City of God, which will consist of all those who desire to be the People of God and who are therefore as beautiful as "a bride adorned for her husband." "He will dwell with them as their God; they will be his peoples, and God himself will be with them; he will wipe every tear from their eyes."[2] This is the gift and the achievement of the Lamb of God, our Lord, Jesus Christ, who offered himself, as an innocent lamb to the slaughter, on behalf of all of us who, redeemed by him, are able to hope for heaven.

A comedy has a happy ending. A marriage *is* that happy ending. But whether in life or in the light of eternity, marriage is a beginning and an ongoing gift as well.

CHAPTER 1

Before Marriage

English is very rich in collective nouns. Everyone knows "a flock of sheep" and "a herd of cattle." We have, of course, "a pride of lions" and "a charm of finches." What is a suitable collective noun for engaged couples? "An anticipation" or "an aspiration" of engaged couples? Perhaps "a promise" of engaged couples. Promise has two meanings. It signifies the hope of things to come—"she is a painter of great promise"—and a decision made, a pledge of future action—"he promised to write and he did."

For this is the time of promise in both senses. It is a sort of lifetime spring. It is full of growing green shoots, buds, and bright sunlight, interspersed with clouds and showers. Life together as husband and wife lies ahead, a short step away. This is a time of looking forward, of expectation and of much activity, but the promise is already there, though it is not yet final. The clouds may sometimes seem thick and dark. Decisions about life in the future can sometimes reveal differences that the couple had not anticipated; that may demand here a compromise or there perhaps a rethinking of plans.

Visiting a large department store with a young friend, I wandered with her into the salon that sold bridal dresses. One wall had on it a huge mirror, perhaps twenty feet square, surrounded by a carved gold frame. We sat for a little time on one of the sofas that stood between the cases of dresses around the periphery of the room. A number of young women came in separately, wearing their jeans and sneakers, with looks of faint anxiety on their faces. They were mostly accompanied by older women, probably their mothers.

The young women disappeared into the changing rooms. Then they emerged, one by one, each dressed in a long white dress of silk or satin, brocade or velvet. They looked at themselves in the big mirror and were transformed. Each young woman carried herself with grace, head high, and with deep seriousness looked to the future and the momentous and happy day in prospect, the gateway to her life with her chosen spouse.

The way they considered their images was quite different from that of a girl trying on a party dress, pulling it this way and that for the best and most glamorous fit. The wedding dress (whether or not they actually chose the dresses they tried) spoke of ritual and destiny in the rite of marriage. "A bride all dressed for her husband."[1]

Does this picture seem alien to contemporary culture? Does it seem to suggest that the bride is too anxious to please or is seen as a trophy or a plaything for the bridegroom? It seems to me, on the contrary, that a truth is being expressed. We "*learn*" people initially through our perception of their physical presence. The bride's attractiveness provides one of the reasons why the bridegroom wants to marry this particular woman in the first place. More than that, she is loved: her fiancé loves her for more than her looks, but he loves her for those as well. "…The bridegroom rejoices over his bride."[2] The way he looks also matters to her; it gives an indication of the sort of man he is. Because we are composed both of body and spirit, we "*learn*" another person through the body, that is, through our eyes and ears. We do not come to know a person as if he or she were an idea, a disembodied thought. We perceive through our bodies, as well as understanding the invisible, spiritual parts of another through our reason and our ability to reach out to the other's essential personhood.

Love is one of the great beautifiers, which is why bride and groom really do always make a handsome couple. On their wedding day, in the church, he looks his best. He awaits his beloved. She advances toward the altar and him, walking slowly, perhaps on her father's arm. They are doing something that is beyond themselves, something that God himself wants them to do and, to use human terms, rejoices in! They are borne up by the rightness of their actions and by the approval given to them by the thousands upon thousands who have gone that way before.

Marriage—Why?

Marriage goes back not only to the first book of the Bible, the Book of Genesis, but also to the mists of time. In recent years, however, an anti-marriage, "it's-only-a-piece-of-paper," "why bother" sort of fashion has arisen. So it is worth considering here the most obvious, least spiritual ways in which it benefits loving couples. These advantages are not widely known. The statistics that support them are often hidden in the pages of specialist journals, and if they make the newspapers at all, they are usually buried at the back.

Experiments in "free lifestyles" and "free love" have been a romantic aspiration of some who saw themselves as "free spirits" way back to the beginning of the nineteenth century. A life unfettered by rules and restrictions has a powerful appeal. However, any such experiment in living has to rely on someone else to pick up the pieces, because one person's apparent freedom is someone else's servitude. An individual who takes up and then discards sexual partners is rather like someone who restricts his or her diet to chocolate cake. After a time, each slice of cake becomes less and less appealing. But in our analogy, each slice of cake stands for a human being, who is devalued and thus has to live with rejection, which is a very hard thing to do. If both sexual partners come to feel that their sexuality is so trivial and value-less that promiscuous behavior simply does not matter, they will fail to give each other a gift of self and their ability to love will become paper-thin. For love is not confined to sexual love; there are many other kinds of love. However, if one aspect of this universal love loses its savor, every other kind of love is affected.

How, then, are married couples better off than those who are not married? The desire to give and receive love is among the deepest desires of the human heart. It is God-given—his gift to his creation—and it is best realized in marriage, which itself mirrors God's outgoing love.

Even with the many problems facing marriage within our society, in fact, there are many signs that men and women were meant to be bound together in love and fidelity. According to research of the literature,[3] conducted by the think-tank Civitas, people in contemporary Western society who are married live longer than those who are not. The psychological and social health of both husbands and wives is better than that of their unmarried neighbors. On the whole, they worry less, they feel less lonely, and they sleep better. Married men living with a wife reveal lower risks of early death and, according to an American study, they are two or three times less likely to die at an early age in comparison with unmarried men. Among married men living with their wives, the rates of death from accidents, suicide, homicide, or cirrhosis (which is usually caused by excessive alcohol intake) were actually three to five times less than those who were unmarried.[4] Marriage appears to have a "protective effect," perhaps because of the emotional support that married couples give each other. So, other things being equal, marriage lets you have a longer and less stressful life, especially, it seems at first glance, if you are male. But women benefit as well.

Two surveys of people's perception of their own well-being were carried out seven years apart (the second in 1993). People who had married in the interval between the first and second surveys reported in the second survey that they felt better in terms of psychological and social well-being than they had in the first. Their marriage had cheered them up, if they had reported lower levels of well-being in the first survey. This was particularly noticeable in women.[5] The Committee for International Cooperation in National Research in Demography reports that a large number of studies have found a relationship between marriage and people's feelings of well-being and mental health This is true for both men and women in the countries studied, mostly in the West, but also in other parts of the world.[6]

A survey sponsored by the United Kingdom government found that men were happier married, but women were less happy married than unmarried. However, this was based on a study of divorced couples![7] Under U.K. law, the wife in a divorce case usually has care of the children and often keeps the house that was the marital home. The husband, of course, is required to provide support for the children, so the wife may feel comfortable with the arrangement. If she was quarrelling with her husband, or tired of him, she might well feel better off. In some cases, the husband may find that he has lost his wife, his home, and daily contact with his children, even without desiring a divorce, while his wife has only lost her husband and retained everything else. On the face of it, and perhaps one should say "at first," the wife may be pleased with the outcome—though equally she might not have wanted a divorce and is likely to have suffered great heartache at her rejection if she were divorced when she would have preferred to remain married to her husband. After the relatively exciting feeling of a new start, the divorcee is likely to feel lonely and to have an even greater sense of her responsibilities, especially where there are children— though no doubt the unintended consequence of the divorce law in the United Kingdom is to weight it in favor of the wife, because of her care for the children of the marriage. Just as all marriages are different, so, one would suppose, all marriage breakdowns are different, but it is hard to feel that one can base an impartial assessment on the consequences of marriage for men and women on research from such a negative base.

Marriage also influences behavior for the good. Fewer married people go to jail than unmarried people. Married couples are better at paying their taxes—though this may not seem a very attractive consequence! They are far less likely to have many sexual partners than people, married or unmarried, whose relationships have, for one reason or another (including death), experienced breakdown. This guarantees that they enjoy better physical health with fewer infections. According to the evidence, they have less cause to report depression, personality disorders, schizophrenia, and drug and alcohol dependence.

Recent research shows some unexpected benefits for those who are married; for instance, married patients are more likely to recover and less likely to die in the hospital after surgery than unmarried ones. The health gap is even seen to be growing between married and unmarried patients in the affluent world, according to a study published in 1987.[8]

An Australian study of over ten thousand adults found that marriage does indeed make both husbands and wives happy (though everyone knows some exceptions to this rule). This is in line with a growing feeling among social scientists that some earlier investigations, which appeared to conclude that married men were happier than married women, were invalidated by either a faulty methodology or a feminist bias. An earlier (1972) study of stress-related symptoms in married couples indicated that wives suffered more stress than their husbands. However, David de Vaus revealed that this study was based on a very narrow definition of stress and omitted alcohol and drug abuse as resulting from stress. His study of the 1996 survey of mental health in Australia found that one in four men and women could be described as unhappy when unmarried. Married women with children (and a job) were the happiest among women.[9]

In the ordinary course of things, marriage gives you someone to share your thoughts, your hopes, and your concerns with. The irritations of the day can be soothed by telling them to your spouse—though it is probably good not to go on too long about them! You have someone who will enter into your excitements—a new job, a promotion, even a compliment. There is someone to go on vacation with, without the anxiety of going away with a friend, who may behave quite differently in a different environment—and in a way you may not like! Husband and wife can explore new places and cultures together, finding out new things about themselves as they interact with new experiences.

Marriage and Children

Fidelity is the solid rock on which marriage is built and should be absolute. In his *Theology of the Body*, John Paul II taught us that fidelity is a necessary part of God's loving plan for us. Sex is not merely a pleasurable activity but a symbolic and nuptial act that consummates—brings to a higher, more perfect level—the relationship between a man and a woman. Without the covenant of marriage and the promise of faithful love to unite them, couples cannot mirror the faithful love of God.

Statistically, however, contemporary society does not rate fidelity as being of the utmost importance. As we've seen, married men and women overall have fewer sexual partners than unmarried ones—and the numbers are not confined to those with a religious faith. The greater the number of sexual partners, the greater the risk of sexually transmitted diseases. One further negative result of sexually transmitted disease, beyond the illness itself, is an increase in miscarriages and even ectopic pregnancies. In addition, in 2003, the U.K. government's chief medical officer informed people of the dangers of such pregnancies after use of the so-called "morning after" pill, which is one of the stratagems for dealing with the possibility of pregnancies that the woman fears (more likely outside than in marriage).[10] Because marriage demands and predisposes men and women to fidelity, marriage is good for the health of both.

A very sad statistic gives the sudden infant death rate as six times greater for babies registered by the mother alone than for those born within marriage.[11] If that reveals a failure of care, we also have to ask who has failed the mother.

Research upholds the commonsense view that marriage provides the best framework for bringing up children. A study of 18,500 babies showed that "children born to single, non-cohabiting parents are the most disadvantaged," and that this continues through life. "The most advantaged children are those born to married parents,"[12] but breakdown and divorce have a deeply negative effect on them. A study by Richards and Dyson in 1982 found that "marital separation is a process with profound consequences for children." Children affected by this often feel anger, directed at one or both parents, sadness, and depression. Younger children often cling to the parent they are left with and regress to the behavior of a younger child. Older children often seek "compensation" relationships outside the home.[13] Children are much less likely to run away from home if the home consists of their two parents who are married to each other. Stepparents, acquired after the breakdown of the parental relationship, are— statistically and in fairy stories—the catalyst for sadness and disturbance.[14]

Children of married parents living together are less likely to have problems of the kind outlined, and they are seen, statistically, to suffer less from psychiatric illness. It seems that the psychiatric problems consequent upon marriage breakdown can last many years.

The offspring of ordinary families, consisting of father and mother married to each other, tend to do better at school and are less likely to misuse alcohol and drugs or get into trouble with the police. With two parents around, it is easier to keep track of children's activities and generally keep an eye on them when they get to the age when they want and need a certain independence. If one parent alone is bringing up the children, that parent is likely to be the mother. However, TV and radio interviews with teenagers caught up in a semi-lawless environment have revealed, more than once, that the adolescents themselves blame their behavior on the absence of fathers in their homes.[15] They feel that there is no figure of authority who cares enough (in their eyes) to make them law-abiding. Their mothers are, perhaps, too tired or too soft. They seem aware of their lack of role models.

Recently published research also shows that where husband and wife live together in the family home, their daughters are less likely to become pregnant in adolescence.[16] In *Animal Farm* terms, we can say, "Two married parents, good." It must also be said, though, that in many individual cases a mother or a father on her or his own is successful in bringing up children.[17]

Cohabitation and Its Disadvantages

The loss of the understanding of marriage as the real scene and context for sexual love has led to much uncertainty and instability. Sex between a man and a woman binds them together, but without the firm commitment of marriage, that bond is unlikely to be sustained. The fracture is likely to produce damaging results for one or both of the adults and serious trauma for any children. The gift of self that each makes to the other in the covenant of sacramental marriage strengthens the couple for the exciting challenge of building a life together and making a gift of their mutual love to their children.

It is self-evident that if, for any reason, a couple who consider themselves in love do not wish to marry, their relationship is more fragile than that of a similar married couple. If one cannot, for whatever reason, commit oneself before family, friends, and God to a real, lifelong, and loving relationship to one's beloved, the relationship is likely to be less committed than a married one. A less committed relationship suffers from uncertain expectations, which may well lead to a high level of tension between the two people in question. This in turn may provoke difficulties between them and also exacerbate the ordinary worries about buying a house, the arrangement of finances, and care and financial support for children. Cohabiting couples are more likely to break up than married couples, especially where there are children.[18]

According to two studies, it appears that married people suffer less depression than those who cohabit. One would indeed expect that the greater instability of a cohabiting relationship would produce increased anxiety, leading to depression. Investigation by the Institute for Social Research found that cohabitation was not, in a majority of cases, seen as a stepping-stone to marriage. Those couples who live together are less healthy than married couples, more abusive to each other, and less faithful. It is not surprising to find that cohabitants also show the highest level of alcohol abuse. Only 48 percent of cohabiting couples studied had stayed together within five years of the birth of their child. With married couples, the figure is 92 percent.[19]

Again, common sense leads us to the same conclusions as research. An "unbound" relationship presupposes a freedom that is not really compatible with security and long-term plans, and implies an imperfect gift of self. The gift of self, as we shall see, is at the heart of marriage. The woman in an informal relationship of this kind might wonder about the future for her children should her partner decide to rupture the link. The man might be concerned about the possibility of losing touch with his children should the partnership founder. Of course, sadly enough, the same events can take place in marriage, but the bonds of even secular marriage are certainly stronger than the wisps that tie informal, live-in relationships together. The partners have to rely on feelings—and our emotions, on their own, are wavering things.

How Did Marriage Get Such a Bad Name?

First of all, nobody can fail to see that in a society that offers so many choices, it is hard to choose the one that appears to be the most demanding. Where marriage is the custom for almost everyone, the path is much clearer. Until the middle of the last century, lifelong marriages were the norm. Since marriage was accepted as the most usual of social arrangements, parents, who were married themselves, had a stronger role to play in guiding the next generation and were likely to influence their children to follow their own example. Until the 1960s, the age of majority was twenty-one. Fewer people went to universities or third-level education colleges, so they entered the workforce earlier and met adult responsibilities at an earlier age. In many cases, they were ready to take on the challenge of marriage, though their horizons were often narrower.

These remarks are very general. Plenty of individuals, at all periods of the twentieth century, followed their own paths for better or worse. However, the numbers of marriages registered reveal that marriage was the common choice during the first half of the last century. Births registered outside marriage were very few in the same period, compared with increasing numbers during the second half of the century.

Many practical difficulties face couples who wish to marry in the climate of the early years of the twenty-first century after Christ. The cost of housing presents a real hurdle; jobs are less secure, and it is usual to enjoy a pleasant, but expensive, social life in the company of many friends and acquaintances. Saving money seems out of the question and living on credit is the usual way forward, especially, of course, for those who have had to incur a high level of debt in order to finance their university educations.

However, lying behind this scenario are several strands of thinking that may have contributed to the current distaste for marriage. Two are to be discerned in recent history—recent, that is, compared with the life of the Church. The third is of twentieth-century origin. All three strands provide some valuable insights, but all three have inherent flaws in them that militate against true growth in the understanding of what it is to be a human being, male or female.

The first goes back to the intense individualism that emerged from the ideas of Rousseau in the late eighteenth century, and a resultant belief in the untrammeled goodness of the "natural man" and the "noble savage." The thinking went: If people were allowed to do what was natural to them and to follow their instincts, the good life would result. Those who currently uphold the notion of "free love" are, in essence, pursuing this belief. It depends on a wholly theoretical view of human nature. Anyone who has tried to organize anything will have found that any two individuals have at least three opinions as to the best way to proceed in a plan of action—and this is often true even of married couples. People's instincts are often in conflict, or at least in tension. The "natural man" comes up against every other "natural man," both male and female. A society in which everyone could pursue his or her own path, irrespective of others and without compromise, would be chaotic. Nevertheless, superficially, the idea has its charm.

The second line of thought is a political one stretching back to the nineteenth century. Political theorists such as Marx and Engels sought to prescribe a comprehensive view of society that would give almost total power to the central authority of a state in order to control individuals and make them part of a corporate enterprise that would, in turn, benefit the whole. There were two different institutions that needed to be destroyed, as these theorists thought, before they could achieve their desires. The first of these was religion, Judaism and Christianity. Judaism suffered, as we know, unbearably under the Nazis, but it also suffered under the Soviets. Similarly, because the aim of the Christian was union with the divine, he or she could not, therefore, accept the claims of the state as the ultimate reality.

The other institution to be ousted was the family with the married couple at its heart, because the family has its own integrity that threatens the hegemony or final authority of the state. Thus, the social theorists downplayed the concept of marriage and the part that women play in caring for their families. They sought to make both males and females equally economic units contributing to the state, rather than husbands and wives, fathers and mothers, working outside and inside the home primarily for the good of the family. These thinkers had no perception at all of the joy couples can find in the home and the family that they create with one another. The family is the home where most people live in the fullest sense. A small boy at nursery school said to me on one occasion, "I like to be at home!"[20]

The third ideology is to be found in the feminist movement. Although the ideas of Communism have been disproved in practice, and communist states have fallen, many women have embraced ideas from the feminist mindset, not merely equality with men (which, as we shall see, is enshrined in the Judeo-Christian teaching) but near identity of role with them—which, in some cases, can lead to conflict between the demands of marriage and family and the pursuit of a career. As society developed, women were right to look for equality with men in rights of education, property, and politics,[21] and in many societies of the world, women are still denied their full humanity. In the developed Western world, women have the same basic rights as men, and yet women who embraced the ideas of feminism saw essential womanhood as a disablement that denied them the freedoms of males. Some women seemed to have lost sight of the understanding that men and women complement, rather than replicate, each other. Where this has occurred, it has led to a widespread perception that marriage is less important than individual choice, and that other social groupings are just as valuable as marriage.

Governments increasingly tend not to support marriage more than other less stable relationships, and our contemporary society does not favor marriage. Meanwhile, the cost of housing, for instance, and young people's debts make it much harder for them to think of marriage as the obvious next step in a relationship. Yet, as we have seen, married couples are good for society and for themselves!

The Social and Personal Benefits of Marriage

The fact that marriage is good for both husband and wife is the basic perception of the vast majority of humankind. Not all marriages are fashioned so as to promote the personal formation of husband and wife. But, as we have seen, in the Western world there are many advantages brought by marriage that are not visible in other forms of social arrangement between the sexes. These are, in a sense, the lowest common denominator of the benefit that a marriage can bring. The sacramental graces of marriage, and the universal benefits of Catholic Christian marriage, will be outlined in the course of this book.

For Further Exploration

1. What do you think would be a suitable collective noun for engaged couples? Why?

2. Imagine a young woman emerging from the dressing room in a long white dress, the momentous seriousness of her face as she gazes at herself in the mirror, the transformation from the anxious girl who entered the store minutes earlier. Do you think all the fuss and the dressing up associated with weddings are important? Why or why not?

3. According to the surveys mentioned in chapter one, there is a definite relationship between marriage and people's feelings of well-being and mental health. Why does it appear from social

studies that married couples do better in terms of well-being than couples who are merely cohabiting? (NB: People who live celibate lives from motives of religious or other commitments are in a different category. There are certainly callings besides marriage in which people can find fulfillment.)

4. How does "free love" fail to live up to its name? What are some of the possible negative consequences of serial sexual relationships?

5. If children are living with only one parent, or with parents who are unmarried, in what ways might they be adversely affected? What kind of advantages do married parents give to their children?

REFLECTION

In your life so far, what has been your attitude to sexual relations outside marriage? With chapter one in mind, consider how your perceptions or acts have affected or might affect your life, your past relationships with others, your relationship with God, and your relationship with your future spouse if you choose to marry.

CHAPTER 2

Preparing for Marriage

The decision has been made and the couple wish to make their vows before God as well as before their families and friends. What is the next thing in the forefront of their minds? It is the reception!

Planning the Reception

What sort of reception do people have? That question is a bit like asking, "How long is a piece of string?" Receptions can be anything from a huge affair, which requires a "party organizer" to arrange it, to a simple meal for close family and friends.

No wonder it is the wedding reception rather than the wedding itself that worries the bride, the bridegroom, and the families! First of all, who is going to pay for it all? The tradition that the bride's parents pay is not current in every family. Nowadays, brides and grooms tend to be older and have probably been earning their own living for some years. The bride's parents' ideas of how much the reception should cost may be very different from the expectations of the couple—or the parents may feel that it is not their business any longer. Not all families, with the best will in the world, can fund the party. These matters have to be teased out gently and considered without rancor. One way forward is for the couple to fund it themselves, accepting any contributions that the bride's family—and even the bridegroom's family, if it seems appropriate—can afford to give.[1] One thing is certain: it is not worth running up enormous debts in order to pay for an impressive reception, nor is it worth it to put off the marriage in order to save just for the party. Saving for the new home is another matter.

I once read a magazine article about how to make your wedding unusual. The writer suggested a medieval theme or something sophisticated and art deco! As if such ingenuity was necessary! As if some sort of play-acting emphasized the truth! As if a wedding required something to spice it up—like the sort of office party where all the guests are bored with each other before they arrive! A wedding has a center, a reason—the loving commitment of bride and groom before God and those they love, be it relations or friends.

A marriage is, indeed, an occasion for celebration, and in some cases it may involve preparing the biggest event the couple will organize in the whole of their lives. There is so much to think about. The dress is a basic concern—antique or modern, off-the-rack or specially made? Is any relation or friend good at dressmaking? Or should it be hired? The headdress—a veil, a hat, a tiara, flowers in the hair—which is it to be? Or is there a family heirloom? A dress sent from the Far East at the start of the Second World War and kept until a peacetime wedding? Does the bride want to follow her grandmother and wear it? (Or would she sooner die?) The bridegroom's suit—formal or informal, "designer" or not, a sober tie, a flamboyant waistcoat? One bridegroom whose father had died wore the suit his father had been married in, which provided a lovely sense of the continuity of families—and it fitted him perfectly.

In times past, a bride, said the rhyme, should wear "something old, something new, something borrowed, and something blue"—old for continuity of families; new for the new life she will lead; a loan that shows her friends are still her friends and will continue to support her; and something blue for our Lady, Mary, the Mother of God, who is the mother of us all.

What about transport? An ancient Rolls Royce (hired, of course)? A horse-drawn carriage? A friend's clean and respectable car? Here the bride's father may well want to have a say. There was an old song that went

> It won't be a stylish marriage,
> I can't afford a carriage,
> But you'll look sweet upon the seat
> Of a bicycle built for two.

On the other hand, families can be difficult! The older generation often has fixed ideas about how weddings should be celebrated. What sort of reception should be held? Endless variations are possible, and all cost more than everyone hoped! A formal dinner is expensive, goes on for ages, and traps people in the company of whomever they have been put next to. It also usually involves an awkward gap between the actual marriage and the reception. A less formal reception is capable of much greater flexibility, both in cost and arrangements, but some people may think it less impressive for their big day. Then there is the cake. Is it to be traditional fruit, marzipan, and icing, or something delicate with fresh fruit on top (which has to be all eaten on the day), or some cake, however bizarre, that one of the families involved always has on grand occasions ("If we don't have it, Aunt Gwenda will be so disappointed"). The rule of thumb, I think, is to accommodate suggestions within reason—though I am not able to define "reason" here.

There are other even less quantifiable worries. Will the two families get along? Will a truce be called on internecine strife? What about the uncle who said nasty things about a cousin? Or the cousin who had a fight with an aunt? What about that awful friend who just has to be invited ? (Every couple has at least one awful friend.) Does one family think itself a cut above the other? It is wise to decide quite firmly about the length and number of speeches in advance. Best men and even fathers of the bride have been known to go on and on, taxing the patience and goodwill of all present. A rule of thumb is the pithier the better. These are real concerns, but one way or another they will be solved.

The grand wedding, though lovely in its way, is not necessarily the easiest start to married life. It can become overblown, and the arrangements and the reception that cause such anxiety and expense can dwarf the actual marriage—really the important thing. A guest list consisting only of close family and close friends on both sides may help in focusing on the reality of the event. There is nothing, after all, to stop the couple inviting all and sundry when they are settled in their home. A hundred years ago, the custom was for a bride to wear her wedding dress on social occasions in the first few months of marriage. Thus she got value for the money she (or her father) paid out for the dress, and she probably enjoyed the kudos of her status. I imagine that today it would attract curious looks, though it would be fun to try.

It is not, however, the Church that prescribes a particular sort of dress or color of dress.[2] For centuries, all but the very rich just wore their best clothes—if they had best clothes.[3] The Church certainly does not say that there has to be a reception or an expensive party of any kind, let alone a honeymoon holiday. She does not insist on flower arrangements in the church, though flowers in church are a hallowed tradition. Wedding rings are incorporated into the wedding ceremony, but the Church does not say that both bride and groom should receive them—nor that they should be of precious metal, though that is what most couples would want. Marriage in Catholic understanding is not a legal arrangement, though it is that as well;[4] it is not just an aspiration, though it includes aspirations; when contracted by two validly baptized persons, it is a sacrament.

Well, What Is a Sacrament?

The first place to look for enlightenment about a sacrament is the *Catechism*, because a catechism is a teaching document.

Catholic teaching is doubly rich in that it refers not only to the Bible as the word of God, but also to the tradition that has been handed down from the time of the apostles. The guardianship of the Church, which was given to Peter as an office, is the guarantee of the authenticity of the Church's central teachings, as coming from Christ himself.[5]

The *Catechism of the Catholic Church* is a comprehensive statement of Catholic teaching.[6] Before publication, the material was sent to the Holy Father, Pope John Paul II, to every bishop in the world, and to all major seminaries for their acceptance, so it stands as a definitive work. It should be the reference book, along with the Bible, in all Catholic homes. The tone of this book does not share the perhaps rather staccato note of the older *Catechism*, which derived from the Council of Trent in the sixteenth century. The new *Catechism* is serene in tone and conveys a gentle confidence. It defines sacraments, with reference to St. Luke's Gospel, as "powers that come forth" from the body of Christ, which is ever-living and in turn gives life. "These powers are the actions of the Holy Spirit at work in his body, the Church. They are the 'masterworks of God' in the new covenant which will last forever."[7] So, the sacraments come from Christ, through the Holy Spirit, to the People of God.

The older *Catechism* defined a sacrament succinctly. It said, "A sacrament is the outward sign of inward grace, ordained by Jesus Christ, by which grace is given to our souls."[8] This is perhaps a rather bald statement, but it is a very clear one. The sacraments bring God's grace, that is God's life, to us through material things, the outward signs—water, oil, rings, bread and wine—along with words. God, who is infinite and perfect and Creator of us and all things, and we, who are created and finite and very imperfect, come together and are joined through the sacraments. It is, to put it in human terms, as if God saw that his creation, wonderful as it was, was not enough to slake the thirst for the love of God in the parched human beings he had made. It was Christ himself who wanted to give us the water of life and wants still to draw us closer to him in our own lifetimes by giving us these means of grace.[9]

The *Catechism of the Catholic Church* indicates that the Church, which is under the guidance of the Holy Spirit, came to recognize and number this treasury of gifts of grace, given to us by Christ himself to increase the life of God within us. That is not to say that the Church changed her teaching—rather, she came to understand in greater depth what the teaching, given her by God to disseminate, really meant: that is, the mystery of communion with God who is love and who is One in Three Persons. Thus the Church came to discern that there are seven sacraments, seven specific means of grace instituted by the Lord, which have special reference to different times and conditions of individual life.

Each of these sacraments stands on its own because of the saving action of Christ through his death on the cross, and each celebration of a sacrament depends on that saving action. In each celebration of each sacrament, there are three dimensions that the *Catechism* brings out (nos. 1122–30). The first is the role of faith; the second, that the sacraments confer the grace they signify; and the third, that they are pledges of eternal life.

The sacraments "not only presuppose faith, but by words and objects they also nourish, strengthen, and express it. That is why they are called 'sacraments of faith'" (no. 1123). By faith we recall the saving work of Christ, but this is not a casual remembrance, like sending someone a birthday card. It is a deep remembering, a bringing to mind that shrinks the perception of time between the moment or action that we remember and the hour when we think of it. We know the importance of this, though sacramental memorial far surpasses it, when, for instance, we remember the war dead on Veteran's Day or bring to mind a precious moment of love or recognition.

"Celebrated worthily in faith, the sacraments confer the grace that they signify. They are *efficacious* because in them Christ himself is at work" (no. 1127). Every sacrament makes Christ's paschal mystery really present to us today. This is not the same as play-acting or the police reconstruction of a crime, which is intended to jog people's memories. In the Eucharist, Christ's sacrifice of himself on Calvary is made again, sacramentally, "in an unbloody manner" through the words and actions of the priest,[10] just as it was made in advance of his death, at the Last Supper, and culminated in his resurrection from the dead. A memorial on its own would lack this immediacy. It would remain in the past, like a postcard from a far-off country. The very heart of the mystery of the sacrament of the Holy Eucharist, the celebration of Mass, is the exchange between heaven and earth. Christ's offering of himself is accepted by his Father, and the bread and wine become his body and blood, soul and divinity.

Finally, the sacraments give us a "pledge of glory yet to come."[11] They remind us that Jesus Christ has gone before us, to prepare a place for us in the eternal banquet of heaven.

Every time, as long as the sacrament is celebrated in accordance with the intention of the Church, grace flows into the recipient, not because of his or her holiness, or even the personal holiness of the celebrant (the priest, in the case of most of the sacraments), but because of Christ's action in the sacrament itself. In marriage alone of the seven sacraments, those who receive it— that is, the bride and bridegroom together—are themselves the celebrants of the sacrament. The priest is the witness.

Whether the sacraments bring forth "fruits," however, depends on the individual, since serious sin makes a person unreceptive to grace. The grace is given, but the individual who receives it cannot open himself or herself to the gift.

The first sacrament to be received is Baptism, which removes all sins, the common original sin of all humanity and (in the case of adult Baptism) sins committed by the individual to be baptized. Infants, of course, cannot commit sin. One who is baptized becomes a new person, an adopted child of God, a partaker of the divine nature,[12] and a temple of the Holy Spirit.[13] This new person, when beyond babyhood, is still subject to temptation but has received the grace to combat temptation when it occurs.

The sacrament of Confirmation, in a sense the completion of the sacrament of Baptism, is a formal means by which the Holy Spirit, the Comforter, comes down on us to strengthen our faith and our resolve to live in Christ, as he did on the apostles at the first Pentecost. With the Eucharist, these sacraments are those of initiation into the Church, marking us with a seal as a sign of belonging. A person's seal is a confirmation of authenticity. Popes and monarchs use their seals to show that a document does really come from them. Baptism and Confirmation establish our initiation and can only be received once because, through them, we are marked with God's seal as his own people.

The Eucharist is the great completion of these sacraments of initiation and unlike the others can be received over and over again. Everything in the Catholic Church is bound up with the Eucharist. In the words spoken by the priest and in the action of breaking the bread, as Christ's body was broken at his passion, the sacrifice of Christ on the cross is made present and relived in an actual not a metaphorical way, but without the agony of pain and loss of blood—that is, sacramentally. On Calvary, our Lord Jesus offered himself to his Father for us—to make good everything that was lacking in us because of our unfaithfulness to the will of our Creator (even though our life depends on him from minute to minute). This offering is made again and again wherever the Mass is celebrated—in a magnificent cathedral or a poor tiny chapel; in a prison or in a palace; on the back of a truck in a theater of war or in the peace and serenity of a convent or monastery; in a football stadium with thousands in the congregation or in a secret place in fear of persecutors. Jesus Christ himself gives himself to us as our food when the celebrant priest says the words that consecrate (that is, make holy) the bread and wine (the "signs" of the sacrament), and these elements are changed into the body, blood, soul, and divinity of Jesus Christ. Those who receive Holy Communion receive Christ himself as his gift to us. The Mass is the Last Supper, the Crucifixion and the Resurrection. This is indeed the "great mystery," not in the Agatha Christie sense of a puzzle with a solution, but in the true sense of something beyond the possibility of our human experience—the exchange between heaven and earth. Pope John Paul II speaks of "Eucharistic amazement," made up of wonder and joy: the very center of the Christian faith.[14]

So that we can be healed and washed from the sins we have committed since our Baptism, God has given us the sacrament of Reconciliation, which enables us, as individuals, to "make up" the quarrel with God, which is sin. God does not pick the quarrel! In his love for us, his creation, he wants us to love him and live in him. Because of our frailty as human beings, we often use our free will to please ourselves in ways that are far from God's ways and that prevent us from growing in Christ. The remedy is this sacrament of Reconciliation, or Confession, where we acknowledge our failings and faults, listing them as best we can and expressing our sorrow for them so that they are forgiven by God, through the words of absolution (forgiveness) spoken by the priest as God's instrument. We then have to accept the penance he gives us (usually some prayers to say) as a sign of our repentance. It is also known as the sacrament of Penance. Whether it is called Reconciliation, Confession, or Penance, the sacrament is the same. It is the best preparation for the reception of other sacraments, including, of course, the sacrament of Marriage.

It is perhaps worth saying that priests in confession come to learn the dark and grimy ways of the human heart, and this enables them to understand men and women with their strengths and their weaknesses. Our secret failings are safe with them—they will never reveal them. Nor will we shock them with the confession of our sins—sins are never anything new. Priests are trained to put from their minds the confessions that they have received. However, if we feel embarrassed before a priest whom we know, we can simply go to another Catholic church and make our confession in complete anonymity.

We have another sacrament of healing, the Anointing of the Sick. This is a specific means of grace for us at our most physically vulnerable time, which comes by means of strengthening oil and consoling prayers. The remaining two sacraments are Holy Orders, by which men are consecrated to the priesthood, and Matrimony, through which the spouses are consecrated to each other through their own act.

The Second Vatican Council (1962–1965) described God himself as the author of marriage, to which he has given its own proper laws.[15] Marriage is the way of life to which God calls the majority of the human race, and it is indeed inherent in human nature, in the complementarity of male and female, which calls out the love of each for the other. We are speaking here of the way in which God created human beings, so that marriage exists at the level of primary longing, before any other kind of social grouping. Marriage predates nations and states, politics and economics, bosses and workers.

Marriage has always and everywhere had a religious element to it, especially in Christian understanding. The marriage of Adam and Eve in Genesis is presented as something directly created, not something that just happened in nature.[16] At the marriage at Cana, Jesus turned the water of natural love into the wine of love in marriage, as later on at the Last Supper he was to turn bread and wine into himself.[17] St. Paul speaks of "the great mystery,"[18] which refers to the relationship between Christ and his Church and between husband and wife. After the time of St. Paul, at the beginning of the second century A.D., St. Ignatius, a bishop, wrote that the consent of a bishop was necessary for Christians who wanted to marry. This was to indicate a difference between pagan and Christian marriage, although the ceremonies, shorn of honor to the pagan household gods, were not unlike.

What the Couple Preparing to Marry Must Do

The first step is to contact the parish priest of the church where one or both live. He will need to know about the two people and their background: their addresses; their religion; when and where they were baptized and confirmed; where they hope to marry, if they want the wedding to be celebrated in another parish. If one of them is not a Catholic but has been baptized in another Christian tradition, the local Ordinary can give permission for the wedding. If one of them has not been baptized, a dispensation has to be asked of the bishop of the diocese, because the marriage will inevitably lack something of the Christian dimension and it may be harder for the Catholic partner to live life as a Catholic. The Church is aware, as the couple initially may not be, that "mixed" marriages can easily result in tensions between the couple, especially with regard to the education of their children. It is important for both parties to consider this before they marry.

They will be asked whether either has been married before and, if so, whether the marriage was celebrated in the Catholic Church or was a civil marriage. If a Catholic contracts a marriage other than in a Catholic church (or, at least, without a Catholic priest present), that marriage is invalid in the eyes of the Church (unless a dispensation from canonical form is given). If a request for marriage comes from a Catholic who earlier contracted a civil marriage, the request must be referred to the marriage tribunal, although in some cases it may be handled by the parish priest. If the request comes from a widow or widower, even if they were previously married in a civil ceremony, the bishop does not need to be consulted. The man and woman requesting marriage are also asked if they are related.[19]

We can see how seriously the Church considers marriage by the detailed questions she asks and concerns she raises. She wants marriages to be good, happy, and loving. It is for those reasons that she expects the couple to attend preparation for marriage that will include the Church's teaching about the sacrament, which the couple may never have heard or may have forgotten. The priest has the responsibility of assessing to the best of his ability whether he is satisfied that the relationship between the man and woman gives adequate hope and foundation for a true and lasting marriage. To do this, he will need to talk with both of them together and perhaps separately as well. He has their good at heart, and he will not be trying to trip them up! He wants their happiness, which means that they will need to think about the issues that will be part of their new life together.

At the end of their formal preparation, they will be asked separately to give their response to certain questions. Each has to say how long he or she has known the other "well"; whether each intends the marriage to be a "permanent and exclusive partnership of life and love, which only death can dissolve"; and whether each intends the marriage to be "an intimate union for the mutual welfare and support of the partners and for the procreation and upbringing of children."

Then they are asked to say that they are entering marriage freely without pressure from parents, the other partner in the marriage, or anyone else. This condition goes back to the early centuries of the Church.[20] Finally they have to affirm that they are sure that they wish to give their free consent to the marriage without any reservations. They each declare before God that they have thought carefully and have answered the questions honestly and sincerely, and they sign the diocesan marriage registration in the presence of the priest or deacon. He in his turn has to state that he is convinced that the two people wishing to marry understand the nature and obligation of Christian marriage and intend to fulfill their responsibilities.[21]

In the case where a Catholic wishes to marry a non-Catholic, the Catholic will be asked to make a promise that he or she is "ready to uphold my Catholic faith and to avoid all dangers of falling away from it. Moreover, I sincerely undertake that I will do all that I can within the unity of our partnership to have all the children of our marriage baptized and brought up in the Catholic Church." How the promise of the Catholic is made in cases of mixed marriages and disparity of cult cases varies from episcopal conference to episcopal conference; all that is required by law is that the Catholic make the promise and the non-Catholic party be informed of it. The priest declares that in his opinion the Catholic will not be opposed in the practice of the faith. Similar investigations are made in the case of marriage with a unbaptized partner.

If the couple wish to marry outside the parish or to invite a priest other than the parish priest to officiate, the parish priest will, at his discretion, arrange permission to do so.

A modest fee will have to be paid to the church, and the parish priest will also tell the couple how to get in touch with the director of music at the church if they want to have music, so that they can discuss what they would like and how much organist's and singers' fees will amount to.

The couple must also apply for a marriage license from their town or city clerk and pay the corresponding fee.

Finally, it is customary and only fair that a donation be made to the priest. He will have put in many hours of work instructing the couple, filling out forms, and making sure that everything is ready and prepared. Factor this into the general budget. One priest said to me that when a couple asked him what they should give, he replied, "About the cost of the cake." Compared with the cost of the whole reception, all these fees amount to very little.

The Rite of Marriage

When both members of the couple are practicing Catholics, the rite of marriage is best celebrated during Mass, the Nuptial Mass. Christ's giving of himself, hidden in the form of bread and wine, is mirrored (though, of course, faintly) in the gift of self that the bridegroom and bride pledge to each other. There are four distinct rites of marriage (Marriage Within Mass, Marriage Outside Mass, Marriage Between a Catholic and a Catechumen or a Non-Christian, and Marriage Before a Lay Minister). For a mixed marriage, the local Ordinary may permit the use of The Rite of Marriage Within Mass "if the situation warrants it" (*Ordo Celebrandi Matrimonium,* no. 36), but the *Directory for the Application of the Principles and Norms on Ecumenism* does not encourage this because the Catholic Church does not have open Communion. The couple will have decided on the music and hymns that they want, and they will have chosen readings and prayers.

The bridegroom takes his place at the front of the church first and awaits his bride. She walks to a place just in front of the altar to meet her bridegroom, with her father or with family members or friends, customarily to the music of the organ or the choir. Or the priest may greet bride and groom at the door of the church and lead them with their family and witnesses up to the altar, while the entrance antiphon is sung (or said) or a hymn is sung.

The priest-witness of the marriage begins the marriage ceremony with the words that serve to introduce and punctuate all the ceremonies of the Church, the sign of the cross: a cross "drawn" with the right hand on forehead, heart, and both shoulders, a reminder of the place where Christ died for us and our redemption was achieved. It is accompanied by the words that indicate our discipleship of the one God in the Three Persons of the Trinity: God the Father, God the Son, and God the Holy Spirit. The priest then greets the bridal couple and everyone present and offers a prayer for the bride and groom, pointing out that marriage is a symbol of the love of Christ for his Church. This is also a mystery, and we shall look at its meaning later on.

As at every Mass, we think for a moment of our sins and failings (not out loud!) and together ask God's forgiveness. Then a reading from the Old Testament or from one of the letters from the New Testament follows, and then we sing or say a psalm. The couple are free to choose from a number of readings suitable for the occasion. There can be another reading, or the priest can go straight on to a reading from one of the Gospels.

After his homily, words of his own on marriage and its importance, the priest conducts the rite of marriage by asking the couple whether they are prepared to make a full gift of self to the other, to love and to honor the other for the whole of life. They respond individually, "I am." They are asked if they will accept children with love as a gift of God—and they answer affirmatively. They state, individually, that there are no reasons why they should not be married, and by name each declares the intention to marry as the Church, who is our mother, demands. Each takes the other, as spouse, with the words "I do."

Joining hands, each of them calls on everyone to witness the marriage and they elaborate their commitment to each other by listing all the circumstances, good and bad, that they will surmount together as man and wife—riches and its opposite, good health and sickness—for the whole of their lives. They then exchange rings, or the husband gives his wife a ring. The gift of a ring underlines the gift of fidelity and love each promises the other.

The prayers of intercession follow. They can be composed by the couple or their friends. The suggested prayers remind everyone of the presence of Christ in the sacrament of Marriage and ask God the Father that Christ's presence will remain active in them during good times and times of difficulty; they ask that the couple will love the children that God may send them and that the children will in turn bring them happiness. One prayer that may be used reminds all married couples present of their own marriage vows and the blessings they have received. The bride and groom may also want to ask for blessings on their families, their countries (if they have different nationalities), their professions, or for their particular concerns.

Then the Mass continues in the usual way with the offering of the bread and wine, and the priest prays for the newly married husband and wife, that as God's love and providence has guided them to come together, he will bless them for their whole lives.

The preface to the Eucharistic Prayer of the Mass speaks beautifully of God as Father of the world of nature and of grace, in which husbands and wives come together in an "unbreakable bond of love and peace." In chastity, their love brings new human beings into the world, to become members of the family of God, enriching humanity and the Church. The word "chastity" in this context may seem surprising, since it is often confused with continence in ordinary speech. Its meaning, however, is concerned with the right use of sexuality in God's plan. After all, it is part of his creation! We will look at the meaning of this in a later chapter.

After the consecration of the bread and wine, and their elevation now that they have become the body and blood of Christ, and after the Lord's Prayer, in which everyone joins, the priest prays especially for the new wife, that she may receive the grace to love and to be a peacemaker, and for the new husband, that he will recognize his wife's equality with him and trust her and love her in the same way that Christ loves his Church. He asks God that they may be blessed with children and live to see their grandchildren. These prayers are preceded by a prayer to God the Father, as Creator, which looks back to Adam and Eve and their union, a symbol of Christ and his Church, and to the survival of marriage, which was not obliterated despite original sin.

If both bride and bridegroom are Catholics, they receive Holy Communion during the Nuptial Mass in the usual way. If one of the spouses is a member of another Christian congregation and would very much like to receive Holy Communion alongside the Catholic spouse, in very limited circumstances this permission can be obtained (as detailed in canon 844). It is exceptional because intercommunion is a sign of unity, which—

alas!—has not yet been achieved between the different Christian communities. It is something to be worked for and prayed for.

People who wish to do so can receive a blessing from the priest as an alternative to receiving Holy Communion, crossing their arms over their chest to indicate their desire.

This exclusion from Holy Communion is often a matter of great sadness for family members who are not Roman Catholics. In one case, it was decided that only the bride and groom, both Catholics, should receive Holy Communion, so that any feelings of exclusion would be diminished. It may be decided that a Nuptial Mass, which of course has Communion within it, is inappropriate. This is something that needs to be lovingly and tactfully explored, perhaps with the parish priest as well as with family members.

The priest blesses everyone there, and the ceremony is concluded.[22]

If the marriage is celebrated without a Mass, all the other prayers and blessings are the same. There are also many different prayers that may be chosen.

For something so momentous, it is remarkably simple.

The Mystery of Marriage

The "mystery" of marriage is so wonderful that it lasts a lifetime. The *Catechism* stresses the good news that God loves us with a love that will never be revoked and that married couples have a part in this love that will sustain and help them. Their own faithfulness to their love for their spouse makes them witnesses of God's love for them, even when times are difficult. There will be times when they have to fight their self-love, for the love of the other. A man and a woman choose each other because they love each other, and they marry because they want to declare this love and this total commitment to the other and to seek God's blessing on their natural and mutual attraction.

When they come to see the priest about their future marriage, of course they have to be free to marry; that is, they cannot be married already. As we have seen, a widower or widow is able to marry again, because death has parted the couple, but someone who is divorced and whose spouse is living cannot validly enter into another marriage. A sacramental marriage that is consummated is for life and is indissoluble. (Although the Church may grant dissolutions in other cases, and situations exist in which one may be divorced with a living spouse and yet be free to enter another marriage validly, as with a Catholic who failed to observe canonical form.) Even if a civil divorce has been obtained, it does not affect the religious standing of the marriage. In the eyes of the Church they are still married. This may appear hard, but it was Christ himself who said it, and in doing so he awarded a much higher status to marriage than his Jewish audience did—and even his disciples were dismayed by the absolute standard he proclaimed.[23]

Why does the Church concern herself so deeply in what might seem to be simply a matter for the two people who want to marry?

The Church is a mother to all her children. Just as a mother—and a father, too—cares passionately about the welfare of her children, the Church cares passionately about the welfare of her offspring in the spirit. A wedding in church is not just the provision of a fitting background for the photographs or the video, but a means of grace for which the couple have to be prepared. As Dietrich Bonhoeffer, a Protestant writer and theologian, wrote to a bride and groom from his prison in Nazi Germany,

> Your love is your own private possession, but marriage is more than something personal; it is a status, an office. Just as it is the crown and not merely the [power to] rule that makes the king, so it is marriage and not merely your love for each other that joins you together in the sight of God and man. It is not your love that sustains the marriage, but from now on, the marriage that sustains your love.[24]

This is an important point. The marriage is something that exists, as it were, beyond the subjective feelings of the couple. It needs witnesses. Even nonreligious marriages have to have witnesses in order to be recognized as legal entities. In a sense, it is objective, not just "all in the mind." It is a sacrament, in which God's grace "solidifies" the feelings of the couple into something as firm as rock. This needs to be reflected in the way the couple look, in the formality of the occasion, and in the words and actions used in the ceremony. Our society prides itself on the frankness and spontaneity of our actions and exchanges. The idea of prescribed and formal words and gestures is largely alien to us. Yet these support and buoy up our intentions; in this case, the intentions are to love, care for, and live with the other for the rest of one's life. Just to say whatever came into one's head would do nothing for an occasion of such significance. (Imagine the banalities, the hemming and hawing, and the awful embarrassment!)

As we have seen, marriage has been weakened by the diminished support of the society in which we live. In Christian terms, marriage is just as important as it ever was. A husband and a wife build a structure, a family, that is good for them and for their children. Marriage binds them, so it is important that they have thought deeply about what they are going to do and the commitment they are going to make. Mother Church wants their marriage to be excellent and so needs to instruct the couple and question them to find out about their perception of what they are about to undertake. That marriage cannot be dissolved, because it has the same faithfulness that Christ shows to his Church. This reference goes back, as we saw, to St. Paul, and it shows how a marriage stretches out so much further than the two people themselves. It has a kind of cosmic importance. Poor Princess Diana famously said that there were three people in her marriage, which made it rather crowded.[25] But where the third person is God himself, we have access to infinite space.

The couple need to get to know each other well and to discover their beliefs, tastes, interests, and hopes for the future. They must be sure that they do not think of getting married just because many of their friends are doing the same. They will be better prepared if they have talked about their attitudes regarding children and how they envisage being a mother and a father. They may well have to learn the rationale behind the Church's insistence on openness to new life. (This does not imply a huge family, which may well not be sustainable in our day and age.) If one party is not a Catholic, he or she will have to consider bringing up children in the Catholic faith and how the parent in question will feel about it. In such a marriage, the Catholic partner is required (and will surely want) to do everything possible to pass on the faith to the children, within "the unity of the marriage." The Catholic parent will also need to teach respect for the other's faith or position.

They should avoid being caught up in the prevalent belief that some sort of trial marriage is a good preparation for the real thing. It is not. It is a bit like going to live in the jungle for a week or sleeping in a cardboard box on the street for a weekend. It is not at all the same as living there forever!

All traditions of Christianity, Judaism, and Islam have always taught that sexual intercourse is for married couples only, and there are good reasons for this. Because the sexual act has the effect of binding the two together, each will also need to be sure that the other will not leave or let him or her down. We have seen that cohabiting fails to provide the stability that both need. Similarly, sexual relationships outside of marriage still feel the need for fidelity and commitment but are inherently subject to fracture and dissolution.

Nowadays, couples also have to think about their careers and how important they are to them. If one receives a very rewarding job offer in another town or another country, how will the other feel and respond? They also have to decide on where to live and what any location means in terms of access to work and pleasant-ness of situation—within the price range they can afford. Taking on a large mortgage obligation early in marriage can prove a very heavy burden.

A Clean Break with the Past

Along with all these necessary considerations and no doubt many others, the best preparation for marriage a Catholic can make lies in the sacrament of Reconciliation. This is the time to look over one's life, to consider its culpable failures, to confess to a priest in order to receive the forgiveness of God (which is mediated by the priest), and to have a real intention of amend-ment. It is the perfect preparation for a new life. The priest will endorse this as most important.

For someone from a different religious tradition, a period of time to look back and express to God sorrow for one's human shortcomings and a new commitment to truth and love is well worthwhile. For someone with no fixed religious belief, a time of retrospection and self-assessment, along with a determination to avoid one's worst faults, would not be wasted and has never hurt anyone.

Preparation for marriage essentially starts way back in the life of the family and in the example given by the parents. Where a family has understood the words of *Gaudium et Spes* (*Joy and Hope: The Church in the Modern World,* a document of the Second Vatican Council) that men and women are really only themselves in self-giving, it is enabled initially to teach even without giving much formal instruction. The feeling in the household, the friend-liness and consideration shown by the parents to each other, the warm but firm direction given to the children, the hugs and encouragement for all, without favoring one above another—these factors prepare children for adult life, in which marriage looms large. In a Christian family, children respond warmly and

excitedly to hearing about the faith. But instruction is also needed at every stage. The child will follow what is good, and with any
hope the things he or she learned as a child will stay with him or
her as a young adult. But as children become adolescents, many
other influences will assail them as they come to live in a wider
world than that of children. Some influences will present, often
attractively, ways of living that run counter to the Gospel. This is
indeed where reason and understanding have to come into play.
The Catholic faith is not against reason—indeed, reason supports
our faith, which is not arbitrary. God does not take the whimsical
actions that characterize the gods of Homer. In the Father Brown
story "The Blue Cross," by G. K. Chesterton, Father Brown real-
izes that the priest he has met is an impostor when the latter maintains that reason is an impossible partner to faith![26] On the
contrary, one has to use reason in order to believe Christian truth
rather than arbitrary assertions. No amount of moral instruction
will give the young a real understanding of life without reverence
for a Creator, because it is only in his sight that the integral value
of life itself and the world is revealed. And what a person believes
and how one lives one's belief will affect a person's whole life—
including marriage. Hence, instruction is essential.

For Further Exploration

1. If you were to marry (or are going to marry), how would
you balance the marriage ceremony and the reception?

2. Consider the three dimensions of a sacrament (faith, the
outflowing of grace, and the hope of eternal life). Within the
sacrament of Marriage, how do these three dimensions work to
bestow the fruits of grace?

3. "It is not your love that sustains the marriage but, from now
on, the marriage that sustains your love." With this quotation in
mind, think about the permanence of the marriage bond and

how it might be a comfort to the couple, to future children, and to society in general. What kinds of preparation are appropriate before marriage, given this serious and lasting commitment?

4. What topics in particular should a couple preparing for marriage talk over together? If one of the couple is not a Catholic, though he or she has agreed to be married in a Catholic church, what other subjects need to be discussed?

REFLECTION

Think of some of the weddings you have attended. Did they serve to symbolize the gift of self that the bridegroom gives to his bride and the bride to the bridegroom? How do you think a couple can focus their ceremony so that it becomes a reflection and a celebration of their future life together within the sacrament of Marriage? Is it significant that the bride and groom administer the sacrament to each other? What is the function of the priest?

CHAPTER 3

Love and Marriage:
The Body in God's Plan

It is sometimes believed that the Catholic Church sees human beings as made up of two opposites—soul and body. The soul, as the spiritual part, is good and can rise up to higher things, and the body is bad and remains like clay, somehow dragging down the aspiring soul like a boot stuck in the mud. This is, in fact, an ancient error and something that the Church herself has never taught—though some of her writers have, at times, come perilously close to affirming it. The earliest evidence for the falsity of this claim comes in the very first book of the Bible, and when Jesus spoke of marriage he referred it to "the beginning," that is, the earliest times.[1] Can we learn anything about marriage from these ancient writings?

God Saw That It Was Good

The account of the creation of the world in the Book of Genesis, the first book of the Bible, is not and is not meant to be a scientific study—that goes without saying. It is, however, a deeply revealing account of God's creative power, which is love. St. Bonaventure, in the thirteenth century, saw that the doctrine of the Trinity—that is, the Three Persons in one God—was as necessary to God as love. God could not love only himself! There is the love of God the Father, the rich source of all that exists, for the Son, who is his perfect image and exemplar, and this love comes through the Holy Spirit, who proceeds from them both and is indeed the love that exists between them. Bonaventure went further, seeing the love between them as overflowing and spilling out into creation.[2] So love is the beginning and center (and will be the completion) of our story as human beings. Again, this is a mystery.

So we can take creation as evidence of God's love. According to Genesis, he judged each category of creation and "saw that it was good." All animals he blessed, telling them to "be fruitful and multiply." Then he created man "in our own image" (note "our," not "my"—a Trinitarian reference); he created them "male and female" and made them masters of all created things. The biblical writer comments, "And indeed, it was very good."[3]

The second chapter of Genesis (considered by scholars to have been written first) describes the individual creation of man and woman. We learn of the life of Adam (which means "man") in the beautiful garden. A river flowed through the garden, and it was full of wonderful plants for food and shade. Adam had every kind of animal to show affection to and also to name. One only has to watch a child choosing what to call a teddy bear to see how important and exciting naming something is. Think of the anxious excitement of parents in choosing the name of their child! It serves to establish the relationship between the named and the name-giver. Yet despite this, the man knew that he was alone, in what Pope John Paul II calls "original solitude."[4] This is primarily the solitude of every man before God. He is conscious of himself, because he experiences his own body. He knows that he did not make himself, and we may suppose that the awe he feels for his Creator is overwhelming. God acknowledged that it was "not good" that Adam, the man, was alone, because no animal could provide the love that he needed, and no soul mate existed for him. No one existed who resembled him and was made in the image and likeness of God; and as he became aware of this, he also

became aware of himself. He was different from the animals in
that he could make decisions and feel the lack of a person to be
his equal.

Thus, immediately after reading the account of creation, we
perceive the deepest need of the human being: to love and to be
loved in return. This need is answered by God with the creation
of Eve, built into a woman, we are told, from the rib of Adam.
When Adam woke from the sleep into which God had put him,
he cried out:

> This at last is bone of my bones
> and flesh of my flesh;
> this one shall be called Woman,
> for out of Man this one was taken.[5]

He is created from dust; she is created from the living creature, though her creation is described in a way that John Paul II
calls "archaic, metaphysical, and figurative."[6] The Bible only
describes Adam as male when Eve has come into being, and
Adam's cry at finding her reveals the flesh and bone identity of
male and female, as well as their difference and complementarity.
Male and female are two ways of being a human being. Each of
them, in the Garden, accepts the other with cloudless joy: this is
the time of "original innocence." They were naked and
unashamed before each other,[7] and no tension or anxiety existed
between the two; there was no bid for supremacy, nor were there
pleas for special treatment. Man and woman are depicted in the
perfection of innocence in their marriage, in the whole reality, as
John Paul II says, "of their body and their sex, which is the pure
and simple truth of communion between persons,"[8] which
conceal within them the meaning of fatherhood and motherhood.[9]

This childlike time is shattered by their sin of disobedience,
depicted as the eating of the fruit of the tree that alone was
forbidden them. Pope John Paul II describes this as the "attempt
to abolish fatherhood."[10] The relationship between the man and

the woman and God had been one purely of love and proper humility before their Creator–Father. We remember that Jesus addressed his Father as Abba, Daddy. Here, they put themselves first; their desires supersede all the gifts God has given them. It is something that we recognize in ourselves, and it took the coming of God the Son, the Redeemer, to save us from the universal consequences of egotism.

Yet the marriage survives and lives on in a fallen time, which at once reveals a pointer toward redemption.[11] After their fall, they continue together, but their disobedience to God has destroyed their innocence, which depended on their good intentions. Their "original nakedness" was part of their whole innocent humanity, not differentiated in any way from their complete openness to each other, but later it became for them a matter of shame. They became self-conscious, and their total self-giving became merely a partial gift, because each was aware of self and the preeminent demands of self. They covered themselves up, physically and emotionally.

John Paul II allies shame to fear before another. It is fired by the individual's need for affirmation and the fear of not receiving it, and it is the body that initially reveals the individual. This new condition of fear is the result of sin, which brings with it an inhibition and limitation of the original freedom of men and women. That original freedom of man is the freedom to give. As the document *Gaudium et Spes* declared, "man, who is the only creature on earth which God willed for itself, cannot fully find himself except through a sincere gift of himself."[12] Making us men and women in his own image, God has given us the gift of life, in his own likeness. In order to be like him, in order to experience happiness, we have to give ourselves in imitation of our Creator.

There are many ways in which we can do this, but none more intimate or complete than in marriage. Each partner loves the other in her femininity and his masculinity, and this goes beyond the physical. But it is also completed in the sexual expression of their love. The sexual giving and receiving between the two, the gift of one to the other, creates a community of persons. John Paul II says that the "nuptial" meaning of the body explains the original happiness of man and woman and wipes out shame. Man and woman are fashioned as they are so that this communion of the two is made possible: they are a wedding gift for each other. This, indeed, is the thing that people long for, even though their longing is often distorted and almost obliterated. That is why marriage is one of the oldest things in the world and can be called the "primordial" sacrament, which goes back to the "beginning."

John Paul II isolates the three experiences that the human beings had in the paradisal garden: original solitude, original unity, and original nakedness—that is, self-awareness; closeness to and fearlessness before the other; a spontaneous giving of the gift of self to the other, which leads them effortlessly to a state of happiness.

Their sin of disobedience creates a barrier between the two. Their original unity is disrupted. They are no longer an innocent gift for each other. Their shame, knowing their nakedness, causes them to hide from God and from each other: they make themselves coverings to hide this new perception of their condition. God tells them how their life will be outside the garden—work and sweat, the pain of childbirth, and inequality of love. It is not a threat but rather a foretelling. Yet these very difficulties that they suffer will help them to grow as persons, learning generosity and restraint, picking themselves up after failure, dusting themselves off and starting all over again.[13] Other anxieties beset them— discord, bullying, and jealousy. The mutual gift and the naked innocence have to be reconstructed, through the grace of God, in the life of the two after their sin. As we read it, the life of Adam and Eve after Paradise resembles the life of every husband and wife in their struggle, despite every sort of difficulty, of external circumstances and their personal weaknesses, to live together as a gift for one another. Where the failings of Adam and Eve are given full rein, men and women find that, although marriage is indestructible, the love between the spouses can die.

In chapter four of Genesis, we read that Adam "knew" his wife. To "know" in this sense refers to sexual intercourse, but it also carries the meaning of recognition, not just as a body but as a whole person.[14] They "know" each other through their bodies. They become "two in one flesh," but they remain separate. From this "knowing" comes the child, and Eve is described as "the mother of all the living."[15] In nature, motherhood is the condition that a woman's body aspires to and is prepared for from adolescence. In St. Luke's Gospel, the women praise "the womb that bore you and the breasts that nursed you"[16]—they are speaking of Mary, in terms of unabashed physicality, for her body's part in bringing the Son of God to earth. When Eve gave birth, she cried out, "I have produced a man with the help of the LORD,"[17] knowing that she and her husband depended on God in all their actions. Both now have new responsibilities, and Adam hears that he has no right to dominate another human being, for the person has a dignity beyond that of the animals—a lesson that every generation of males since has had to learn.[18] All women have to learn to give as well as to feel love, which husband and children need to receive. No generation, no individual, is more than partially successful in these demands.

To love is not just to like, not just to feel affection for, but deeply to want the good of the other person. What is the opposite of the verb "to love"? An obvious one is the verb "to hate." There is, however, another word that indicates something which can be in some circumstances almost as destructive as hate—the verb "to use."

What makes humankind special among all the other orders of creation? Plants have a more developed life than stones, animals than plants. Animals are often seen to understand certain human actions and even needs (think of guide dogs for the blind, for example). But it is not just the fact that animals can't cook that reveals their difference from human beings! The difference lies in the self-awareness of the human being and his (and, of course, her) ability to use reason in an abstract way; to speculate about ideas and courses of action; to compare and contrast; to imagine; to respond to beauty in ideas, in persons, in art, in nature. As John Paul II says, "Inner life means spiritual life. It revolves around truth and goodness."[19] The person has close links with things in the external world and asserts his position within that world. He can think and he can choose because he possesses what we call free will, which makes him, whether male or female, a man, with his own autonomy. But what do we say about marriage in this context? In the sacrament of Marriage, in which the bride and groom are the ministers of the sacrament to each other, the gift that they give to each other is not just a ring of gold or platinum, but themselves. The gift of self is inherent in the sacrament—man to woman, woman to man—and this gift must be without limits of time, space, or inclination. It rules out "use" of the other, in the sense that the person is manipulated or bullied into being an instrument of the other's desire, whether in the matter of sexuality or in other parts of life. Between spouses, this principle is important. In their loving interplay, in whatever area of their life together, they have to keep as a ground rule the equality and autonomy as a human being of the other, so that that person is never only a means to an end.

"To use" is to employ someone or something as a means to an end. This, of course, can be an entirely ethical thing to do. If an employer pays a proper wage, the employee accepts that he or she has to do the work that the employer directs him to. Indeed, when employer and employed agree about the value of their joint enterprise, the "common good" can be enhanced. This is true in many other instances of social deployment and action beside the world of work. But what the worker is told to do must be appropriate—if the boss told him to lie down in the road despite the possible traffic, the employee would of course be right to refuse. Nobody can be asked to do something that would forfeit his or her life or damage him or her in a grievous way. In short, there are limits to the demands that an employer can make, and these must conform to reason and to acceptance of the essential autonomy of every man. This is also true even in something like a religious Order, where if the abbot told the monks to go into the garden and eat worms, they would be right, despite their vow of obedience, to refuse.

In marriage the good of the spouse is always paramount, and the good of both parties is wrapped up in the good of one. This may well be difficult to achieve, but to "use" another person goes against the reality of love, and it underlies many failings in marriage; the urge to make use of the other has to be fought. We are human beings and we must expect to fail, but a knowledge of the places where we are most likely to trip is a help in avoiding the unexpected step on the stair.

The Indissolubility of Marriage

We have looked at what was meant by the phrase "in the beginning" that Christ used in his discourse on marriage.[20] He explained that marriage, from the beginning, implied a total and unlimited gift of self and therefore could not be dissolved, even though Moses had given his people a concession with regard to divorce "because of your hardness of heart." Now that Christ had come, with his gift of grace and with his promise of salvation, such a concession was no longer necessary or possible. The "gift" once given cannot be taken back; and man, male and female, becomes the visible, bodily sign of the truth and love of God in his plan. The body becomes a sacrament—a sign of grace.

If "no divorce" seems a very hard saying to a twenty-first-century audience, it was a blow even to the disciples of Jesus. The debate of that time was between two schools of religious thought in Judaism, one of which maintained that burning the soup (presumably on a regular basis) and carelessness in household management was enough to warrant divorce, while the other said divorce should be permitted only for serious offenses like adultery. In each view, we are looking at the initiative of the male. When Jesus was asked by some Pharisees, who were the religiously educated, whether he held that it was against the Law to divorce for minor reasons, Jesus answered that husband and wife "become one body," united by God in their marriage, and are therefore indivisible whatever the circumstances.[21] This, commentators recognize, is the moment when Christ instituted marriage as a sacrament rather than a legal arrangement. The disciples grumbled at his words, saying that, in that case, it was better not to marry. But Jesus said that it was only some people who could live life on their own, and every sacrament through God's grace brings its own power to human endeavor: "For God all things are possible."[22] In this context, the words imply a reconstruction of marriage after the loss of the "original innocence."

Jesus was not just being hard on people. He was saying what marriage is and what that implies for husbands and wives. The mutual "gift" lifts both spouses onto a different plane, where even sadness, some loneliness, and much irritation can be subsumed into love—a deep wish for the good of the other.[23]

From "knowing" each other in the biblical sense comes the child, and the parents come to know each other in their child. The shape of a woman's body, the cyclical nature of her fertility and infertility, and the varying levels of her different hormones are all arranged for the achievement of motherhood, from adolescence to late middle age. This is evident and is not a matter of faith, just observation.

Another human being, made, as Christians believe, in the image and likeness of God, comes into the world by means of the exact development intended to bring this new person to birth. As soon as sperm and ovum fuse, the new being, soon to be "he" or "she" (even before implantation in the womb), is given its first and best present, an immortal soul. It will inherit characteristics of color, height, intelligence, from its parents and from other fore-bears as well, but the spirit is a direct gift of the Holy Spirit, the breath of immortal life. That life can now never be finally snuffed out. Its mortal life can be ended all too easily, but its spirit is there forever.

Man, as male and female, becomes newly aware of his humanity in mutual love and care for the child. The state of parenthood brings an acute awareness of death and the fragility of life. It teaches both man and woman the effect of the corruption of original innocence and that the mixture of good and bad in man can only be explained by this lapse. Man and woman are forever painfully, but also with joy, refocusing their orientation to goodness.

Genesis, of course, presents a prescientific vision, but though it does not describe the workings of the body or the development of the individual, it tells much that is true about man. John Paul II, who coined the beautiful phrase "the theology of the body," says that it must be the context of life and behavior to all men and women.[24] Love is something unique to persons, because it comes not only from the sexual "urge," as it does in animals, but from decisions of the will, which can exist only in human beings. Sexuality, as part of the human makeup, cannot range wildly and without control over society as a whole. Relations between men and women need their own proprieties and restraints—like any other strong emotion. Women do not want to be trifled with, let alone assaulted, but all men are not rapists on the prowl. The committed love of husband and wife provides the right ambience for the sexual expression of that love, bringing them together in closeness and pleasure, and the outcome of that sexual expression is, other things being equal, a new human being in the image and likeness of God. The child anchors the parents' love even more strongly and helps them to keep their sexuality for each other.

Infidelity is also a crime against the child of their love. Is any sexual fling, which leads to the breakdown of trust, worth the loss of those daily smiles and hugs that are the particular joy of a family?

The Greeks Had Four Words for It

In the English language, we have only one word for "love" as a noun, plus the word "affection," which indicates a milder feeling than love. As a near-synonym for the verb "to love," we have only the verb "to like." Though similar, "liking" is not identical with "loving" and is a matter of feeling rather than concern for the other person who is loved. Love is widely and casually used of ice cream and television soaps, as well as of another person—the object of our outgoing concern. The ancient Greeks, on the other hand, used four different words to cover four categories of love: *eros, storge, philia,* and *agape.*[25] Does that matter to us in the twenty-first century after Christ? It can, I think, assist us in a simple analysis of what love is. Love is so important to us that we are, as it were, dazzled by it and find it hard to think about what constitutes it.

Sexual love is not the only kind of love. Nevertheless, as we have seen, the attraction that a woman feels for a particular man whom she has seen or a man for this woman who has just passed by is a mysterious thing. Physical attractiveness is an important part of it, but this attraction is an individual thing and people do not always agree in their perception of physical beauty; what attracts one may leave another cold. Is it something in the expression of a person's face, the way he or she moves, but above all perhaps the way this person talks—nothing to do with accent or fluency, grammatical correctness or streetwise chat, but something indefinable that leads one person to think that he or she would like to know the other person better? The current popular term for this is "chemistry." Chemistry, however, submits to analysis and is confined to material elements. The spark between two people does not submit itself in a similar way. If the other person feels the same, we are witnessing the first manifestation of *eros,* the Greek name for romantic and sexual love. This, in our culture, is the primary step toward a loving marriage.

This feeling may develop into a fascination with the other. The thought of that person takes up much of their time. They want to hold each other, kiss and embrace. Meetings are longed for, are pleasant and exciting, and the two are on the way to being in love. Their love, in time, leads them to see the possibility of a shared life together. They begin to want to commit themselves to each other for good. Their marriage, then, is the great adventure in which body and spirit come together in the fulfillment of their love for each other.

Why wait for marriage? is the contemporary question. There are many answers that will arise in the course of this book, and as we have seen, all Christian churches have traditionally upheld the teaching that the full sexual expression of love is for marriage.[26] But in this context, the reason for keeping full sexual expression of love to marriage is the fact that it is overwhelming, bringing the two to a closeness that they both need to be able to rely on. Without the commitment of the marriage vows, sex is the flashy wrapping paper with no gift inside. That is why rejection by a lover is so desperate an experience, especially, perhaps, to young people, who rarely have the confidence in themselves that they try to parade. In addition, while the man might be able to walk away from a sexual encounter relatively unscathed, a woman may find herself with child. Contraceptive failure is not infrequent. An abortion takes a real life.

The adjective "erotic" in popular speech has come to represent sexual display or arousal. But *eros* involves much more than that, incorporating the other elements in romantic love as well—the tenderness, the excitement, the mystery.

The downside of *eros* is sex for sex's sake, without love, without commitment, without grace. One cannot look at television or read a newspaper without coming across instances of this—often presented as a great good. But it is sex trivialized and diminished.

The narrative of marriage continues, and the word *storge* indicates the special and protective love that parents have for their children. This is probably as intense as the love the parents feel for each other and is necessary for the proper nurturing and development of the young. That is not to say that if the child is denied this intense nurturing love, perhaps because of the death of a parent or even abandonment by mother or father, the child is doomed. Many children who have suffered in childhood grow up to be good and successful human beings—but they will have had much to conquer. *Storge* also reflects love for children within the family, which is such a natural thing that it is almost universal. Children, however much they are loved, can still be intensely annoying or unattractive at any given moment. However, in most cases they are still loved, even when the parents are tearing out their hair with irritation and frustration at whatever it is their offspring are up to.

I once heard a mother say, "My children are one of the best things that has ever happened to me—and I can't stand them a minute longer!" Conversely, the love of parents can become unbalanced and obsessive, which, of course, places a real burden on the child. This rarely happens with a large family, not because the love is like a cake that has to be divided equally, but because the interaction of the siblings gives them room, metaphorically, to breathe! They are not likely to be stifled individually by excessive attention.

Love within families shows many different faces, and *storge* also reflects the sort of comfortable love that married couples often reach after many years. It may look boring to the young, but familiarity and kindness can be the solace of old age. Courtesy is important here. Long familiarity can produce a sort of brutality if it is not countered by loving politeness.

The third type of love is called *philia* and indicates an outgoing affection that binds people together outside their families. It is very important to the time of late childhood and adolescence. It enables individuals to try out their ideas in a friendly arena and helps them to turn toward the wider world. Genuine goodwill is a very attractive attribute and reveals a care for others in a spirit of friendship. Someone outside the immediate family can be a great help in times of tension and difficulty in the family. A charming literary example of *philia* is the Edwardian children's book *The Wind in the Willows,* in which the animals exhibit great camaraderie and care for each other—not least in "taking in hand" the boastful and ebullient Mr. Toad in an attempt to save him from himself![27] In a heroic context, we have the band of brothers of the Fellowship of the Ring, in J. R. R. Tolkien's epic *The Lord of the Rings.* There is, however, a slight danger in the power of such friendships in that a group ethos may develop, which can grow into a herd instinct and override individual conscience.

Agape is the greatest kind of love. It is not self-seeking; it involves a complete self-giving. This is the kind of love through which a man lays down his life for his friend. The death of Jesus on the cross is the supreme example of *agape;* he laid down his life not just for his immediate circle but for all humanity, from the "beginning" to the end of time. His command to us to love our neighbor as ourselves means that we are to try to achieve this very high ideal. This is also the ideal of love in marriage that couples need to keep before them.

It is important to be aware that there are other kinds of love beside the erotic, which seems to dominate the consciousness of the age. There can be a sort of progression from *eros* to *agape,* taking in the other categories and yet living them all simultaneously as well as possible.

Within marriage, *eros* initiates the relationship, which comes to incorporate the special love for the children. As one's children mature, the parents' love for them has to take on a different form. Children have to be permitted to make some decisions for themselves, to choose their own friends and activities (within limits). If parents, and perhaps especially mothers, went on loving and caring for their children as they did when they were toddlers into the time of adolescence, the children would be damaged and stunted.[28] The friendship of others enriches and supports the family, and all the time, with prayer and reflection, the utterly self-giving love of husband and wife grows and brings them closer to God himself.

In the end, even marriage passes away. Jesus makes it plain that there is no marriage in heaven.[29] That is why marriage itself can be a sort of idolatry if it is divorced from the love of God. In *Brideshead Revisited,* the novelist Evelyn Waugh makes his flawed Catholic heroine say, as she rejects marriage with her divorced lover, "I can't shut myself out from [God's] mercy. That is what it would mean, starting a life with you, without him."[30] Marriage itself would become an idol.

What Is It All About?

Do we dare for a moment to imagine, as if we were children and without disrespect, a dialogue between the members of the Trinity—God the Father and God the Son with the Holy Spirit—way back before time began? We have to use human language for this, so the nearest we can get to the mind of God is by analogy, which is a sort of "as if." So we imagine the three Persons knowing their overflowing love for each other will flow out into creation as they enumerate the wonders of creation-to-be: sun, moon, and stars; seas, mountains, plains, and rivers; trees, plants, and the humble grass; creatures of all kinds, fish that are to swim, animals going on land on four feet, birds able to ride the air. These created things will have their own lifespan, but the Persons do not propose a one-shot creation of the things of earth.

The things they will make are to carry on through time. So into their creation God places the power of reproduction to them in pairs (for the most part), so that each species can continue through the ages—though in time some, like the dinosaurs and the dodo, will die out.

But then, to continue our child's view, we imagine the Divine Persons saying, "What of the one we are to make in our own image? Let us make him not one but two, who can love each other with a reflection of our love, but with the difference that through their bodies they can join with us in the creation of another person. This will not be a direct creation, like ours, but using their bodies they will love and embrace and beget a child, who will be in our image and in whom we will breathe our Spirit. Their children will be human beings like them, from the first moment of their life in the sheltering womb, with an immortal destiny and the ability to mature, to find others to marry and produce children in their turn. And this to the end of time. We will love them and they will freely love us in a universe of beauty and love." One of the names of the Holy Spirit, the Third Person of the Trinity, is "Gift."[31] As the theologian Janet Smith defines it, sex is for bonding and babies.[32]

There is a point to this imaginary tale, and it takes us back to philosophy and the question "Why?"

Since God is the creator of all things, everything in creation has a place and a purpose, even though we may not understand it. Food and liquids are for nourishment, for even if we were healthy, we would die without them. In the rich West, there is such an abundance of food that we often forget its primary purpose, and its taste becomes all that matters. We can be sure that people in countries poorer than ours are well aware of the "end" for which food was created. Similarly, we need rest and sleep; the purpose is refreshment and renewed vigor. The most far-reaching and amazing outcome of sex is a new life, and though the mutual love, pleasure, comfort, and release are also part of it, the partic-

ipation by the couple in creation outshines any other aspect of a
sexual relationship. Marriage is the best environment for the
growth and development of the child. Yet it often seems as if, in
the minds of many people, sex has no purpose except pleasure,
and procreation is mostly an outcome to be feared. Young girls are
encouraged to "go on the pill," and boys adjured never to forget
a condom. Yet to follow nature is to know that sex is the mechanism for new life. For married couples, the sexual expression of
their love and the pleasure that they feel binds them together and
helps them to remain faithful to each other.

Sex considered solely as a means of pleasure reveals a very
new attitude among the mainstream of society; even a hundred
years ago, most people in the world would have thought it strange
and perverse, though they would have been aware of a substra-
tum of men who "took advantage" of women.

Priests who prepare couples for marriage have told me that it
is almost unknown for a couple in such circumstances to say that
they do not wish "to accept the children that God sends them,"
as the rite of marriage beautifully puts it.[33] The wish for children
is a deep, natural desire within human beings, though in a social
climate hostile to family life, it is easily obscured. A great generosity can grow out of the love of a young woman for a man and a
man for a woman. They want something to come out of their
love, and the outcome, the fruit, is a child.

From the point of view of the married person, do we dare
attempt an answer to the question "What is it all about?" by
speaking of God's love for us, our love for him who made us and
through his Son redeemed us, and our love for our husband or
wife that enables us to bear the fruit which is the child?

What About Unmarried People?

There is a paradox here. It has been said that an age that does
not take marriage seriously is an age that does not take the conse-

crated celibate life seriously, either.[34] Both paths have as their goal and direction a life focused on God. At their best, both ways are committed in humility to the same end. We have to acknowledge a seriousness in them, which paradoxically again enhances their cheerfulness, their laughter, and their sense of fun. It is not, however, only those who are married or in religious Orders who are able to live their lives with the God-directed love that animates those they encounter daily. Every follower of Christ is enjoined to follow in his footsteps "in the world," whatever one's state of life. People who accept and live Christian teaching are always great examples to others. They are the men and women who can be relied on, who are valuable friends, and who are often able to enrich others with their generosity, their enthusiasm, and their interests. This is seen in particular in the "Little Way" of St. Thérèse of Lisieux and also in the way of St. Josemaría Escriva, the founder of Opus Dei, who promoted and taught a method for a way of life that sanctified life "in the world."

The Incarnation and the Sermon on the Mount

If we need more proof of the goodness of the body in God's creation, we have only to think of the Incarnation. This quite astounding fact, that the Son of God became a man, shows beyond any doubt that a body reveals in itself the goodness of material things and that in the human person the body as well as the spirit has its own value. For this reason the Church teaches that, at the end of time, we will be restored to wholeness with the resurrection of the body. Without the Incarnation, there would be no saving act of Christ re-actuated in the words of consecration at Mass, at that sacred moment when Christ's words and actions at the Last Supper with his friends, the words that are the precursors of his giving his life on the cross for all humankind, are spoken by the priest: "This is my body, which will be given up for you," and then, "This is the cup of my blood, the blood of the new and everlasting covenant. It will be shed for you and for all, so that sins may be forgiven."

The teaching of Jesus, especially in the Sermon on the Mount, reveals his humanity as well as his divinity. He knows the concrete situations in which men and women find themselves—how easy it is to be proud; how often we are downtrodden. He recognizes how we are tempted to give up; he knows our desire to be merciless when we have the power, to give in to impurity when so many others do, to use strife to assuage anger, and to give in when sanctions threaten our religion. Christ's sermon mirrors the Ten Commandments of the Old Testament, but substitutes "Thou shalt" [be happy when...] for the old warning "Thou shalt not" [do...].[35] Each clause is both an exhortation to courage and faithfulness in the face of the inevitable opposition to the good and also a promise of reward; each clause begins with the words "How happy are...." He also demands that we fulfill not just the letter but the spirit of the law—which is a much wider remit and often a much harder injunction. As he says in the teaching that follows and provides an exegesis on the Sermon on the Mount, it is not just that you may not kill; it is that you may not be angry, you may not insult or abuse "your brother"—and we are all part of the same family.

Jesus' first encouragement is to the "poor in spirit" with the promise that "theirs is the kingdom of heaven." The opposite characteristic of poverty in spirit is pride, the pride that led to the original disobedience and that can so easily tempt us to choose ourselves instead of God and ourselves as objects of our love instead of others. This has a particular resonance in the experience of married couples!

He says the pure in heart are happy (or blessed).[36] He follows that up in his further teaching by repeating the order, "You shall not commit adultery," adding, "But I say to you that everyone who looks at a woman with lust has already committed adultery with her in his heart."[37] This is, indeed, draconian. But the truth of it has to be admitted. It is not only in physical action that we can do wrong. The theater of the head provides the stage on which many bad acts are performed. Every action, good or evil, begins with thought. Indulged fantasy can lead to action, but even without the act of adultery, adultery of the heart is still a denial of the gift that husband and wife have given to each other in marriage. Fantasizing about other sexual partners will diminish the exclusivity of the relationship. Though it is not as damaging as adultery itself, it is, nonetheless, a move away from truth, and it is truth that will set you free.[38] John Paul II describes lust as a threat to the whole structure of "self-mastery."

"Blessed" or "happy," said Jesus, "are the peacemakers." There is often room for peacemaking between married couples! If you forgive others their trespasses, God will forgive yours! A "trespass" is some sort of violation of another's space or property or rights.

In the day-to-day compromises of marriage, forgiveness by the one evokes forgiveness in the other. There is a catch phrase that goes: "Love is never having to say you're sorry." Quite untrue! The one we love most is the one we can hurt most—and sometimes do. Never to ask for forgiveness is the mark of the psychopath.

Jesus tells us not to give up or cave in the face of persecution, because "your reward will be great in heaven." Our life here on earth, even within the commitment of marriage, has always to look forward in love to its final purpose.

Marriage is often viewed by contemporary eyes as something humdrum, boring, old-fashioned, and even eccentric. The writings of Pope John Paul II, in particular, illuminate for us an entirely different picture—one of beauty, of ancient promise, and of one of the greatest blessings of God to the entire world in terms of the creation of man and woman as gift to each other. And this gift, like a stone in a still pond, produces circles that spread wider and wider. The most personal of loves has the broadest of contexts.

For Further Exploration

1. How do we know from the study of the Scriptures that Christianity does not deny the goodness of material things, including our bodies?

2. Men and women complement each other. What does that teach us about the sacrament of Marriage?

3. What does the story of the fall of man in Genesis tell us about human nature in the present as well as in the past?

4. How did Jesus teach us that marriage is indissoluble?

5. What are the four different kinds of love? How is each one an important part of married love?

REFLECTION

We know that food is for nourishing us, sleep for refreshing us. What, in God's plan, do Christians believe that sex is for? Is it for recreation and feeling good only? Is it for "bonding and babies"? How does that belief imply love?

CHAPTER 4

Male and Female

The way we look at people comprises, in a manner that we are not always aware of, a whole series of predispositions—our culture and education, our religion, and our philosophy of life. But whatever our perceptions, we can most probably agree that when we walk down the street, when we go to a party, when we look at crowds pictured at some great event, the individual faces and bodies that we see highlighted are all different! We are immediately aware of their individuality. It is quite exceptional to mistake a stranger for someone we know, even though time takes its toll and youthful beauty matures into—well, a face molded by experience.[1] Identical twins are a rare exception to this. People, individually, have a personal cast of feature, a body shape, and a way of walking, let alone a way of talking, that is unique.

The Recognition of the Sexes

What we recognize almost at once about people is their sex. We can tell whether they are male or female. Admittedly, from time to time, in an age when male/female markers are sometimes obliterated by identical trousers and length of hair, whether very short or very long, we may have to look twice. But it is rare to have to look three times. Psychologists Marcus and Overton found that children as young as three to five years old could identify dolls as being like boys or girls on the basis of their hair and clothing.[2] An Italian lady, a friend of mine, knew a little boy who had such beautiful blond curls that his mother could not bear to cut them off. By the time he was three or four, his hair was down to his shoulders. In, I suspect, the absence of his mother, my friend teasingly asked the little boy, "You have such lovely long hair. How is anyone going to know that you are a boy?" The little one thought for a moment and then said, "They'll look at my shoes!" And, as it happens, he was right, because even boy toddlers have, on the whole, larger feet than girls of the same age. With toddlers, the clothes make the (future) man/woman. They are less persuaded by physical differences!

With adults in our own time, the reverse is more likely to be the truth, yet in fact we make few mistakes. We certainly do not need to see them naked to perceive their maleness or femaleness.

Differences Between Males and Females Other Than the Sexual Organs

In general, though there are many individual exceptions, males are taller and bigger-boned than females. Their feet are commonly larger. They have greater muscular development and are physically stronger. They can carry greater weights. One of the reasons adduced by the army for using only male soldiers in the front of the fighting was that a 125-pound woman soldier would not be able to carry a 155-pound man if he were wounded in battle. It is noticeable that you do not see women furniture removers alongside the men who lift vast wardrobes and dining room tables up narrow staircases and around little corners. Nor, come to that, do we see women ballet dancers heaving up ballerinas, let alone male dancers, to twirl above their heads. Men's hands are bigger, and women's, being smaller, are more suited, we may think, to delicate tasks. Men have facial hair, women do not, except perhaps for a few as they advance in age. Women's bodies are more rounded, the breasts and hips curved, the arms and legs characteristically more cylindrical in shape. It is also true that men and women vary enormously in size and there are many women who tower over their menfolk, but overall we observe that men are larger, taller, and stronger than women. Their voices are lower in tone and, in the ordinary way of things, they carry further. One thinks of the breed of sergeant majors who could be heard from three miles away. On the other hand, operatic sopranos in Verdi or Wagner might be able to run them close—though their achievements require dedicated study and much personal talent. All these attributes are subject to variation and training, but, overall, these differences can be seen everywhere.

Differences in Young Children

Very young babies have, of course, no sense of personal identity anyway, and it is even hard for an onlooker to decide whether he is looking at a boy or a girl in the cradle. However, by six months, it is possible to know for certain. Boy babies' features are often larger than girls'; boys are frequently more active or restless, but can also cling more to their mothers. They are often slower at talking than girls and by the age of two can be, according to one commentator, more aggressive and violent than at any other time in their lives! It is as if they do not know what to do with the vastness of the emotions they experience. This is particularly so if they feel they have been frustrated and treated badly by not being permitted to do something that appeared to them to be very inviting—male toddlers, in particular, are always exploring and are notoriously unimpressed by hazards of fire, flood, boiling kettles, and sharp knives. Parents have to be particularly firm and careful at this stage.

It is very instructive to watch small children playing. From a very young age, we observe girls playing imaginative games, creating a world around them. A toy manufacturer remarked that little girls like to create an imaginary something indoors, like a house, while boys prefer to play outdoors. Girls like to pretend to be princesses, mommies and daddies, or when they are a bit older, doctors and nurses. I remember an occasion with a large family when the youngest girl, perhaps aged three, wanted them all to play families and told the two big brothers (around eight and ten) that one was to be Daddy and the other Father. I cannot remember why she thought they were two different people. Perhaps she remembered that the parish priest was referred to as "Father." Either way, the brothers tied themselves together with a skipping rope to the tearful chagrin of the small instigator of the game, who called to them despairingly to "play nicely!" They were ruining her fantasy.

Boys use fantasy too, but often in a different way, as part of a game with arcane rules that often involve chasing and catching and falling over each other. There is, somewhere in it all, an intention to win and be leader or top dog, but it often happens that nothing is resolved and the roughhousing goes happily on, whatever the limits established in the course of it. On occasion, girls can enjoy joining in with this sort of game, but it is often for the fun of playing with others rather than an actual concern for the outcome. Boys, however pacifist their parents, will make pretend guns out of anything.

I once read of very politically correct parents who were determined that their daughter would not suffer the disadvantages of her sex and therefore would not allow her to play with dolls, in order to avoid any feminine bias. She was, however, observed by her grandmother putting two of her building bricks in a line, placing a smaller brick on top and saying, "Baby tired now; go to bed." A young friend of mine, tongue three-quarters in cheek, said to me about her daughter, "We did all the right things; we put her in jeans from day one, and as soon as she could talk, she said, 'I want to wear a pink dress!'"

Should We See Male/Female Differences as Cultural Ones?

Strenuous attempts have been made in the last century to establish that gender identities are made culturally and not inherited as part of the genetic makeup, and sometimes these researches have been in the service of the "new ideas" about women. They appear initially to have been grounded on the behavior of certain primitive tribes, but even then, as Richard Gross comments on the work of Margaret Mead, the researchers sometimes revised their findings radically under the influence of their own personal experiences. According to Gross, after Margaret Mead had given birth to a child of her own, she accepted the role of nurturing as "natural" to women, a position she had earlier rejected—and though we cannot be sure that it was her own experience that changed her mind, it appears to be a reasonable inference. Other studies have relied on evidence of the abnormality of sexual organs and the sexual "realignment" of certain unfortunate people suffering from these abnormalities, in order to seek to establish that sexuality is not necessarily fixed. Still others refer to certain tribes in which some males choose feminine roles. Whether these patterns of behavior derive from hormonal imbalance or psychological bias is uncertain, but there are obvious methodological difficulties in arguing from the rare to the commonplace. It is, I understand, accepted by anthropologists that there is no known society of whatever level of development in which the women alone do the fighting.[3]

There is, indeed, almost as great a variety in the behavior and development of individual boys and girls as there is in the faces we see in a crowd, and St. Thérèse of Lisieux said that souls are as different as faces. Nevertheless, most parents recognize that their babies soon develop tastes and interests that fall broadly into boy and girl patterns. Many parents, like my friend whose daughter wanted to wear the pink dress, try strenuously (or jokingly) to run counter to what are generally seen as boys' or girls' toys. But although many toddlers enjoy playing with anything new, whether considered the sort of toys boys or girls like to play with or not, they often revert to their usual toys in the end, though there are many subdivisions of taste. Much as I have loved being a mother, I remember that when I was a child I had no time at all for dolls but loved soft animal toys. Dolls were always too rigid, and there did not seem to me much one could do with them (so unlike babies, I have since learned): perhaps my animals were further from the real world and therefore better suited to fantasy. It was somehow easier to imagine life in a cave as a bear than to imagine a life in a house untrammeled by the regrettable real-life necessity of parents. It is noticeable that today's parents are more often concerned about their daughters' choice of play activities rather than their sons'. Possibly only a very old-fashioned father would worry if his three-year-old son liked to pretend to be doing the ironing! Most would see it as a useful future skill for the boy to learn. An androgynous ideal is the current fashion, a sort of sexual "middle way," but it seems likely that most boys and girls remain firmly fixed in their tastes, even before the age at which the distinguished psychologist Kohlberg held that children had any awareness that they were permanently male or female.[4] It does seem, therefore, that sexual identity is fixed long before any serious cultural influences impinge on the child.

Different phases certainly exist, revealing different sorts of behavior in the course of growing up. Many a ladylike twenty-year-old has evolved out of a ten-year-old tomboy (even Jane Austen, at the end of the eighteenth century, mentions this phenomenon[5]), and a shy young boy may yet turn into a confident actor or a political heavyweight. Aristophanes in Plato's *Symposium* declared that originally there were three sexes: men, women, and hermaphrodites. The last of these were an amalgam of male and female, with four arms and legs and two faces looking each way. They were globular in shape, and if they wished to progress at speed they did it by rolling over and over! When Zeus decided to curb them by slicing each in two, they simply longed, each of them, for their other half![6] Does this reveal the complementarity of the sexes?

There are many fascinating theories about the factors of heredity and environment and about the sexes, their differences and similarities and how they relate to each other. Nevertheless, the commonsense view—that there are certain differences that are universal, inherent, and not merely learned, and that transcend differences of cultures—has much to recommend it.

It is commonplace in psychology to admit that as soon as one has made a statement about human beings, one has to modify it, if not contradict it outright. One cannot study human beings as if they were shells or plants. So it is necessary to say that the differences between males and females can be modified by the environment and that individual experiences—social attitudes, education, technical discoveries, diet, and so forth—affect everyone.

In addition, each individual's characteristics have what some psychologists term a "shadow image." Carl Jung named the masculine principle the *animus* and the feminine counterpart the *anima* and held that an individual encompasses both.[7] We are not all 100 percent red-blooded men or totally feminine, motherly women. We all have in different amounts masculine and feminine elements, whether we are male or female. Indeed, it would be intolerable if we did not! We would be cartoon versions of men and women, crude and unvaried. It is the moral strength of a woman and the gentleness of a strong man that add to the roundedness and complexity of human beings. Many differences between men and women are indeed the result of education and environment. The biological differences, however, are not only basic to the sexes and not simply confined to genital differences, but they affect men and women as human beings all the way through their lives, like the lettering in the center of seaside rock.

Even if they submit themselves to genital surgery or modification, if they were born male or female, that is what they are and will continue to be, no matter how they choose to dress or whatever sex they consider themselves.

Christianity's Acceptance that Men and Women Are Equal Before Judgment

Christianity acknowledges the natural status of woman as equal (though not identical) to the man in the sight of God and the man as equal (though not identical) to the woman. Edith Stein, a philosopher in Germany in the early twentieth century who died in Auschwitz and who is now a saint, writes in a striking phrase that "salvation admits no difference between the sexes: rather, the salvation of each one and their relationship to one another both depend on the same close personal union with Christ."[8] Woman's equality with man was not perceived in the ancient world or in the world of Eastern religions. Beyond the Genesis text "Male and female he created them," we remember that Christ came to earth as a baby, helpless and dependent on his mother, and that his mother was not a goddess but a human being. That tender image of mother and child was pictured everywhere as the centuries rolled by, and women recognized their own dignity because they shared Mary's womanhood; thus liberated, many women gave their lives directly to God with a sort of abandon and are recognized as saints.[9]

Physical Development in Men and Women

Puberty is the only major physical change that every male encounters. His voice breaks, he starts shaving, and he becomes capable of fathering a child. Thereafter, his physical entity is complete, and he has, other things being equal, only to face the gradual slowing down of advancing age. There is no physical basis for "the male menopause"—though from advertisements one sees practitioners selling nostrums for this nonexistent condition. The male, once adult, does not have a fixed time for participating in the conception of his children. For the woman, it is very different. Her eggs are in place at birth, and from puberty until menopause in late middle age she has the possibility of bearing children, though this finishes well before the likely end of her life. (Very old mothers would never have the energy to bring up their children and would be likely to die when their children were still young and had need of them.) During her reproductive years, she undergoes a cycle of preparation for the possibility of conception every month, and if no baby is conceived, the cycle has to be completed and her womb made ready for the next cycle's possible conception. Her body is continually preparing for the possibility of new life, whether or not she is focused on it intellectually or emotionally. Within the period of four weeks or so, she has different hormones predominating at different times, so that, even if she is in good health and suffers no pain, she may well experience varied moods—sometimes up and sometimes down, triggered by these chemical variations as well as by all the varied facets of her life! Yet it all has a purpose. Her husband will do well to factor in these changes into his understanding of his wife, or he may come to see her as sometimes moody or difficult! Her body makes great demands on her, which can be said to "center" her within it. Her feelings at any one time affect her whole person; anxiety or stress can affect her cycle of fertility. She learns to control these feelings, though not necessarily obliterate them, often through motherhood, because the demands of her baby are even stronger than the demands of her own self! Her bias to nurturing helps her to turn outward to others, even if she is not physically a mother. She "finds" herself most profoundly by reaching outside herself.

A man does not have to accept these kinds of disruptive change to his body, but he may well find other difficulties. Because his person is continually directed outward (however much he may love his home and family), he may find it hard to admit the limitations of his body and intelligence—especially in the company of others. Men are often afraid of revealing their weakness. They often feel that they need to be marching forward with plans and projects, and the inevitable, even occasional, failures are often very hard for them to deal with and difficult for them to admit. I think it is this anxious reticence that often makes women see their husbands as the little boys they once were! Husbands and wives have to try to learn to trust one another with their secrets. Acceptance of a spouse's anxieties is one of the bedrocks of marriage, and the gentleness of husband to wife and wife to husband is probably the most important of all qualities in a marriage and makes for a continuing love. Many polls asking husbands and wives about their first requirement in a spouse have come up with kindness as the most desired quality that they look for. The secrets of married couples are not only those of sex but also those of weakness, and few things are more destructive than the use of confidences as a weapon against the other. The closer each of them comes to Jesus Christ, the closer will their relationship be to each other.

Their Intelligence Is Equal but Different

Intellectually, neither sex is superior, though some people think that it is possible to argue that each uses the brain in a different way or uses different parts of the brain predominately. Of course, there are many different considerations to take into account here as well, including the fact that historically some men have had much greater opportunities for intellectual education and training than women have had—I stress "*some* men," because we have to remember that, throughout history, the vast majority of men had no more opportunities for study than women had. Universal education is a recent wonderful development. In the United States, for example, reformers such as Horace Mann advocated free public education in the mid-nineteenth century. The movement gradually spread, and by 1918, all the states had laws ensuring free public education for children.

The current educational system in many countries aims to free girls from any sex bias in their upbringing, and they are strongly encouraged to study whatever boys seem to be best at—notably, sciences. Many girls, as soon as they are offered a choice, prefer the study of literature, the arts, media studies, and so on.

Although there are always exceptions, for the most part, young girls appear to have a greater facility for describing scenes and persons than boys have, and they learn to speak and read more quickly, while boys seem to understand abstract concepts, like mathematics, better. This may be modified by adolescence, but throughout their development, girls in general respond to arts subjects with greater interest then boys do, whereas boys enjoy scientific studies, solving problems, and observing concrete results. They are also good at abstract thought, whether at chess or in philosophy. Girls may tend to lose interest in sports at adolescence, whereas boys might continue enjoying both playing sports and watching them. This, again, is a very broad generalization, with many exceptions. As previously noted, early preferences are often modified in adolescence and certainly do not imply that men and women cannot equally achieve excellence in the sciences, humanities, and arts.

Currently, the education systems in the United States and the United Kingdom seem to be focused on an assumption that girls and boys should have the same interests and that both should like the same subjects. If boys enjoy a subject like engineering, the educator's object is to make girls interested as well. The hope is that every job largely chosen nowadays by boys should have girls employed in similar numbers, even if girls, given a free choice, might not choose to study that subject. It appears to me that the vision that girls are currently presented with can be hostile to their best interests. They are effectively told that their lives are only to be validated by work in competition with men. This means in effect that as young women they could devote themselves probably for many years to trying to win unnecessary battles and prove themselves better than the men at any job they do.

Competing within the workplace is not necessarily the most important thing for either gender; success in such matters as conquests in war and the making of money is not the criterion for the good life for any Christian. We must follow Christ, who came "not to be served but to serve" (Mt 20:28). To serve God and other people must be our primal goals. We must follow Christ. All other successes are secondary.

Feminism in the last century has been determined to eradicate what feminists call "patriarchy"—power exercised by the male over the female. Certainly there have been cultures, still existing, that deny women any sort of personal rights or autonomy. However, in the Christian West, even as long ago as the Middle Ages, well before the Reformation, that has not been the universal experience.[10] The holiness, that is, the wholeness of women (the two words are cognate)—especially Mary, the greatest of all human beings and a woman—was recognized and highly honored as a result.[11] Many young women as early as the second century gave up their lives as virgin martyrs rather than take pagan husbands with whom they would have to deny their Christian faith; they wished to give themselves directly to God. Their religious faith liberated them from the absolute submission to their fathers and husbands common in the world of Rome and Athens—an amazing reversal of the common culture. Their generosity and love of Christ led to their martyrdom. During the early and Middle Ages of the Christian era, women often enjoyed great power as abbesses of double monasteries, as administrators of their husbands' estates (which were effectively little towns) while the men were away on campaigns, as litigants and followers of trades, as writers and copyists—the latter often in religious houses.[12]

Secularism and feminism have sought to downplay the home and its magical qualities of shelter, of safety, of warmth. The natural affection that women and men have always felt for their children and their spouses has blossomed by the fireside.[13] Men and women both truly need the human warmth of home. However much they have to be out of the house for their work, home remains a special place. As the little boy at nursery school said to me, "I like to be at home."

More Differences

Men and women appear to look at the world around them in different ways. The man will often look to an object, or a result, in a straight line from thought to outcome. A woman tends to look around to see the matter in context and in particular considers the effect that any action will have on others. Women are sometimes called "people people." They are comfortable building bridges. Their concerns are often with others, while men are often focused primarily on the matter at hand rather than on the effect the action will have on others. The diversity and complementarity of men and women enable their children to grow up with a better understanding of humanity in its richness and generosity as well as its failings. Where love is the basis of family life, children have the best chance of maturing as they grow. As with everything else to do with people, however, there are exceptions. Married parents have their failures, and many single parents raise well-balanced children who grow into generous adults.

When a married woman meets another socially, she will usually first ask about the other woman's husband and children, friends and cats. The other woman will reciprocate. They will discuss their families' health and the triumphs or tribulations of the children before turning to other concerns (single women will ask about each other's affections and the state of play). A man, equally devoted to his family, is likely to discuss outside concerns with a friend—business, sports, or politics, perhaps—first. Sometimes, he will be just going out the door when he remembers to ask about the family. The other man may respond, "Fine. How is yours?" And the next minute they have parted. When there is something specific to say, men will interest themselves in it, but women will nearly always start a conversation with inquiries about personal relationships. If a woman says she has a headache, a man will often respond by saying directly, "Have you taken a painkiller?" A woman will reply to such an announcement by saying something like, "Oh, I know just how you feel, I had the most horrible headache last Tuesday." And only after that does she say, "Can I get you something for it?"[14] She will tend to ask, "Can I get...?" He will say, "Have you taken...?" It is useful for both parties to know that these responses are equally characteristic, to be accepted with understanding rather than with annoyance. Both can smile and say, "How typical."

Carrie Paechter, in a book called *Educating the Other,* is quoted as suggesting that women use what she terms "troubles talk," where they support each other by discussing matters of concern to each. The provision of a forum for this expression of solidarity and friendship is, Paechter writes, sometimes more important than the provision of an actual solution to the problem at hand.[15] There is a good deal of truth in this. Some problems are insoluble, some disappear by themselves, but the ability to share them with other women is a great help and a solace. I once was a witness of this strategy in action. I heard a woman say to her friend, quite crossly, "My husband's been away, but he is back tonight and I've been trying really hard to make everything just right. And when he comes in the door, I bet he notices the one thing I haven't managed to do." The other woman said, "It is exactly the same for me. I put flowers all over the house to welcome him home, and the first thing he says is, 'I see you haven't fed my winter cactus!'" Both women laughed delightedly and cheered up.[16]

The seeming abruptness of some men is no matter for criticism. Ordinarily, men must continually engage primarily with the further world, whereas often women, even if they are business leaders, take on the role of the parent who most often addresses the family's needs in an immediate way, keeping tabs on all the things that make up the life of the household. This is not to demean contemporary husbands, who are often very good at playing a part in domestic matters and in the care of children, and who are likely to be good at minding the children and at holding the fort in any domestic crisis. However, women have had a symbiotic relationship with their child for the nine months of life in the womb, and the close dependence of the one on the other has a lasting effect. However much both parents share looking after the children, at least in the early years, the mother is closer to her baby than the father is. His time will come later, when, alongside his wife, he introduces his child, boy or girl, to the outside world with games and hobbies and by providing in himself a model of how men are. "Isn't Daddy fantastic?" said one not-yet-three-year-old when his father returned from a business trip.

The adolescent boys who hang around some densely populated parts of our big cities in gangs, making life unpleasant for others, often lack fathers living with the family in the home. They miss the positive view of the male—someone at once strong and familiar, someone to look up to. It has also recently become apparent through research in the United States and New Zealand that the absence of a father is a factor in the development of girls, too, though not simply because of poverty or high levels of stress in the home. The study suggests that the father who is present is able to teach his daughter, by example, how to behave across the sexes in a nonsexual way, where sexual behavior is inappropriate. Because she is proud that her daddy loves her, she recognizes where reticence is necessary. She knows that she is already loved by one man.[17]

Sharing a Life

Married couples have to learn to live together in harmony—the spontaneous joy of being in love will not last forever—and it is very unlikely that the harmony of their life together will ever be perfect or complete. They are two in one flesh, and yet they are also separate. They have married because they love each other, are attracted to each other, want the good of the other, and want to spend their lives together—and yet there will almost certainly be times when they feel alienated, irritated, lonely, and dispirited. It seems to me that if we need evidence of the fall of man, we can find it in the inability of men and women, so obviously meant for each other, to live easily in mutual harmony! St. Paul knew all about that, though he was not referring to marriage when he wrote, "I do not understand my own actions. For I do not do what I want, but I do the very thing I hate."[18] Each person has so many facets, so many layers of personhood—some strong, some fragile—that for each to accept the vagaries of the other day after day is a hard task. Like St. Paul, we mean to do well but are easily thrown off course by being hurt or irritated, annoyed or bored. Are there remedies for this?

The first remedy lies in the relationship that each has with the heart of Jesus, the paradigm of generous love, and this requires the prayer of loving and humble talk to him—raising up the mind and heart. Husbands and wives must also remind themselves that they love each other and that they have made a gift of themselves to one another in marriage; any feeling of superiority or command must transform itself to that of service. The belief that God loves each of them and wants them to love one another can ground their relationship. It is worth remembering again in this context the words of *Gaudium et Spes,* which states that man (both male and female) is the only creature on earth that God wanted for its own sake, and therefore we must deduce that man can fully discover his "true self" in giving himself. God, our Creator, *gave* us ourselves and made us in his image and likeness. We have to try to be like him in our creative giving, whether as man or as woman.[19]

"Love does not consist in gazing at each other, but in looking together in the same direction."[20] On the strong basis of loving the other in Christ, it is often at its best when the two of them stand side by side, with some project in mind—even if it is only planting the garden or planning a birthday party.

As we have seen, one of the most noticeable of women's abilities is that of building bridges. Because of their concerns with family and friends, with people, they prefer in most cases to link rather than to sever. With their husbands, they may do this in a rather roundabout way, avoiding direct confrontation. It may be irritating, but it can be successful, and spouses may be helped to edge to a solution instead of a confrontation. The husband may learn that his wife's approach to problem solving takes account of more elements in the story than his own more direct methods give space for, though it can cause irritation. On the other hand, man's ability to cut through a problem and come swiftly to a decision is essential for the ordinary living of life. It is useful to be able to distinguish the characteristics of women and men in this field, and to realize that both have their own validity and neither should be dismissed. Nor are these traits universal; many a happy marriage has been lived by a meditative, even vacillating, man and a decisive, even bossy, woman. Perhaps most couples alternate their behavior, effectively taking turns to see the best way forward in the face of life as it is lived.

When real difficulties occur, when hard decisions have to be made, the only way forward is that of tolerance, affection, and

courtesy. If the couples have established a habit of praying together, a joint prayer, a committal of the issue to God, is probably the
best of all ways to start. Because he created us, he wants us to
acknowledge the relationship with him, whatever our troubles. I
believe firmly that prayer assists in the next most important
requirement, and that is courtesy. Courtesy is not the same as
distance or lack of sympathy. It implies and reveals the respect
each spouse has for the other; the service that each offers to the
other. It may be difficult to learn, but it is invaluable once it is
learned.

> Of Courtesy it is much less
> Than courage of Heart or Holiness
> Yet in my walks it seems to me
> That the Grace of God is in Courtesy.[21]

It involves acknowledgment. I was once in a shop when a
young couple came in. I did not know them well, but I knew
they were close to each other. The girl was eating a muffin or
something similar, and I imagine her boyfriend had asked for a
piece. She tore a bit off and half turned to give it to him, without so much as a glance in his direction. She did not seem particularly angry or sad, just cold. It was rather chilling and
discourteous, and I was not surprised to hear later that the relationship had not blossomed and they were apart.

A clear head is also necessary, because in serious matters it
may well transpire that one spouse or the other has to give in, has
to agree to a decision that will affect them both in very many
different ways, and has to accept that the other's concerns in this
instance must be paramount. The more complicated and fraught
contemporary life becomes, the more these issues need to be
faced bravely. The marriage itself is so important that both parties
will need to bring honesty and love to hard decisions, within, as
the law of the Church says, "the unity of the marriage."

Marriage is a thing-in-itself to be accepted as paramount
between the spouses; it is the bedrock of their life together. If they

have entered the marriage seriously, taking their vows for real, they will know that each will suffer through any rift—let alone what their children will suffer. Each, therefore, also has to check his or her behavior almost on a daily basis—what is called the "examination of conscience"—measuring their own conduct against both their direct relationship to God and the well-being of the other. This is not scrupulousness, just common sense. The trick, I suspect, is to share as much as one can and to accept that men and women are both human and different and that husband and wife are individuals, as well as being two in one flesh.

John Paul II says in his apostolic letter on *The Dignity and Vocation of Women* that the male's tendency to dominate is a result of the fall and that "this domination indicates the disturbance and *loss of stability* of that *fundamental equality* which the man and woman possess in the 'unity of the two,'"[22] the disharmony that we, as human beings, brought on ourselves by our disobedience to God, in choosing our own will instead of his. This is something that each individual man has to struggle against—not least within his marriage. But woman, too, can misuse her qualities, by expecting too much of her husband, demanding too many things, too easy a life, or by pursuing her own interests too exclusively to the exclusion of her husband; in addition, she may seek to dominate him and deny him his role as husband and father.

St. Edith Stein makes plain that a husband also has to make sure that his wife's gifts are encouraged and honored by him, so that she is not confined "to a sphere too narrow for her talents," which could lead to their atrophy and the lack of enrichment of her spirit.[23] She needs time (that precious commodity) to express and develop her talents, whether in the professions, business, or the arts. Both husband and wife are to imitate Christ, understanding that each can lead the other and each must submit to and honor the other for the good of both.

Despite all these caveats and stern admonitions, husbands and wives, through God's grace, have lived good and happy lives together down the ages. They have found love and fulfillment growing through the years to old age, relishing the success of their marriage, the high points of their lives in business or professions, accepting that failures are inevitable, watching with pride and affection as the lives of their children and grandchildren, their nephews and nieces, unfold. As for the difference between men and women, let us say, "*Vive la différence!*"

For Further Exploration

1. Think of some of the differences between men and women. How far do you think these are influenced by social conditioning?

2. In what ways is a man's way of talking sometimes different from a woman's? How might it be helpful for couples to be aware of other modes of communication and habits of speech?

3. *Gaudium et Spes* tells us that men and women can only discover their true selves in giving themselves. How does this apply to a newly married couple?

4. Pope John Paul II wrote that there has been a loss of that fundamental equality that the man and the woman enjoyed in the garden described in Genesis. How can husbands and wives try to regain it?

REFLECTION

Consider how the mutual love of husband and wife is likely to change and develop during the course of their married life. How might those ideas help a couple to take a long view of marriage?

CHAPTER 5

Openness to Life

"Are you ready to accept children lovingly from God and bring them up according to the law of Christ and his Church?" This is one of the questions in the rite of marriage that is put separately to the bride and groom during the ceremony. Each must answer, "I am." It is the last of the three questions asked of them. As we have seen, first the couple's freedom to enter into marriage has to be stated. Next comes their firm resolve to love and honor each other for the rest of their lives.

The third question brings God himself into the marriage. It is he who invites the two of them to become part of his creative work in the world, through the sexual expression of their love for each other. When a child is conceived, at the very moment of conception, God gives that tiny one an immortal soul, even while the little body is growing and developing within his or her mother. What in the world could be more amazing than that—except the fact that it is also normal, commonplace, universal? We have to make an effort to stand back and observe what this really entails. Within the Trinity, we see the Father as the one who gives life, the Son as image of the Father, and the Holy Spirit as the love between the two Persons, who is love-as-Person. In marriage, in a way that is reminiscent of creation, the father generates life outside himself, the mother generates life within herself, and the child is the new life that results from their loving act. In an earlier chapter, I fantasized a conference within the Trinity before the beginning of time, in which the three Persons decide that the creation of man, as male and female, would continue through the loving gift of husband and wife to each other, his gift direct and going out from himself, hers receptive, nurturing, and sustaining, which jointly bring the triumphant appearance of a new life—to the greater glory of God! Of course, this is an analogy; who can know the mind of the Trinity? Nevertheless, when we look at the idea of the Trinity, we can discern that all human action follows it in some way. There is creative thought (the Father); simultaneously there is action (the Son); and the fruition (the "Holy Spirit who proceeds from the Father and the Son").

However, the child is not the only gift that God gives in marriage, because the love of husband and wife, expressed sexually, binds them together. The philosopher and theologian Janet Smith describes, in a recorded talk, how she would like someone to write her a rap on the two great themes of sex in marriage, bonding and babies, because, at any one time, if you don't have a baby you have bonding, and you have bonding when you have a baby! It is something to sing about.[1] In a sense, the bonding comes first, to prepare the future parents for the baby, but this does not mean that the husband and wife have to enter into a long apprenticeship in order to bond! It just happens through the sexual expression of their love, in which each has to consider the other. The bonding also continues after the time for babies. But the baby is at the center of the picture. The baby cannot be denied.

The generosity of God is mirrored in a small way by the loving acceptance of children by spouses in marriage. We must also applaud the generosity of many single mothers who fight for their baby's life in the face of opposition from boyfriends and others and who do not give in to the simple, though disastrous, solution of abortion. Children are a gift rather than a frightening obligation: God's love places the little ones in our arms, and we can offer them back to him because we are aware in this dramatic way of his love for us.

Husband and wife form a "dual unity," which, in a sense, reflects the "dual unity" of Christ, who is both God and man and who, in turn, is part of the ultimate difference in unity, the Trinity of three Persons in one God.[2] Love is the attribute that forges this chain.

Because that startling harvest of sexual love—the resulting human being, the child—is made in the image and likeness of God, that baby person will be part of the parents' lives until death parts them (even in the sad cases where a child dies before the parents or walks away from them never to be seen again in this life). So it is that the deliberate denial of this relationship, of parents to child, negates the clear plan of Almighty God, first spoken in Genesis, when God told all creation to "be fruitful and multiply, and fill the earth and subdue it."[3]

Yet many people in our society have come to see the baby as the downside of sex, the hazard against which they fortify themselves regularly by latex or chemicals, copper or plastic; and if the baby arrives in the womb in spite of their best efforts, he or she is often removed and denied the chance of life. This attitude is so entrenched in society that one can imagine that couples today might exclaim, "How can the Church possibly mean what she says, that contraception and birth control are against God's plan for the human race? One would end up with families running into double figures. It is completely impossible! Every child should be a wanted child; babies are pollution. We can't afford another baby, we haven't the room, we haven't the money." And the woman may add, "What about my career?" But wait! Although, as we have seen, children are at the heart of marriage, spouses who accept this entirely as true may indeed find that they have to consider, after the first baby, whether, for serious reasons, they need to wait before another baby is conceived. They can do this by learning the nature of fertility in general and the wife's specific pattern of fertility and infertility in particular. In fact, a woman's egg can only live for twelve to twenty-four hours in her cycle. In the presence of good mucus, the sperm can live from three to five days, so that the fertile time lasts from six to eight days in any one cycle. When she has learned to manage her cycle of fertility by understanding it, along with her husband and with his cooperation, they do not need to resort to drugs or barriers to space their children or to decide when their family is complete.

As people who believe (and on good grounds) in a Creator God, we can see his purposes in many things. Because of the "aboriginal calamity,"[4] the first disobedience of man, we live in a world that is far from perfect, but one that also challenges us to take responsibility for our lives in an adult way, responding always to God's loving request that we should love him in return for his great love for us and that we should seek to live that love in the ways that he commands us. His teachings come through the Scriptures and through the Church. Because he knew that his followers would be imperfect, Christ gave us his Church to be the guardian of his teachings until the end of time.

Openness to Each Other

Human weakness leads us to selfishness and solipsism. It is all too easy to erect barriers between husband and wife. Latex condoms, of course, do just that and are not, in any case, totally effective in preventing pregnancy or avoiding sexually transmitted infections.[5] They do, however, provide a false sense of inviolability, which can lead to a lowering of personal standards. Abortion becomes a necessary backup. Every form of contraception puts a barrier—latex, chemical, metal, or plastic—between husband and wife. The husband refuses his wife the physical gift of himself by literally imposing a barrier, as if he wore earplugs to make himself permanently deaf to her. The wife refuses to receive the gift of the whole self of her husband by some inhibition on acceptance, making herself sterile, as if she had had her lips stitched together so that she did not have to talk to her husband.

Most husbands and wives, I imagine, have no idea that this is what they are doing. Many men may even feel that they are being a support to their wives by not risking a pregnancy.

The contraceptive pill, which "tricks" the body into thinking that ovulation has taken place, can also be an abortifacient—like intra-uterine devices and other implants—which prevents the fertilized egg, the blastocyst, the new human being, from implanting in the wall of the mother's womb. Implantation is also known as "nidation," which means "nesting." In those cases, the baby is denied his nest and thus his life. The "morning after" pill consists of a very high dose of the contraceptive pill that, if it works at all, always causes an early abortion. If it does not expel the new human being, it carries the risk of ectopic pregnancy, which is a pregnancy developing in a place other than the womb. This can be very dangerous for the mother. The morning-after pill also carries a risk of severe, painful, and distressing side effects, and statistically the woman who takes it may well not be pregnant. Conception can occur only during a small part of the month.

The contraceptive pill runs exactly counter to the promise of bride and groom to accept the children that God sends them. Far from being accepted, they are destroyed.

There is a body of evidence that appears to link abortion with the onset of breast cancer, especially in the cases of women who have not had a full-term pregnancy before an abortion is induced. The likely reason for this is that in early pregnancy there is a high level of a hormone called estradiol, which stimulates breast growth. In a full-term pregnancy, many of the cells mature, and this leads to a reduction in the risk of breast cancer; but where the pregnancy is terminated, the cells cannot come to maturity, and that is where the risk lies. Cancer research apparently accepts a link, according to a report in the *Catholic Herald*.[6]

The birth control pill, known widely as "the pill," is a daily pill that contains hormones that prevent a woman from conceiving by keeping her body in a mimicked state of pregnancy. This mimicked state of "pregnancy" will never go to term. The risk associated with the birth control pill may be less than that associated with the morning-after pill, but the two are not dissimilar. Many other risks are associated with the pill, including strokes and heart disease.

The Catholic Church exists to love and value God-given human life. Therefore, she cannot possibly sanction any act that militates against innocent life, from conception to natural death. The whole of creation is fashioned in order that the glory of God may increase, and men and women are part of that purpose. A mechanistic understanding of human beings is inadequate, and an understanding of human life in the context of God's creation leaves no room for any separation between the unitive and the procreative in married couples.

Christianity and Contraception

Since the belief in contraception as the essential liberating tool of contemporary life is widely prevalent and, at present, many governmental campaigns promote it, it may come as a surprise to many to learn that until 1930, all Christian churches were totally opposed to it. They held to the Judeo-Christian tradition that sex was meant for the procreation of children, as well as for pleasure and comfort, "the bonding" of the spouses. This was the traditional teaching, though it is true that some theologians saw the temptations to which sex can lead at least as clearly as the good it can bring, and took a gloomy view. Quite apart from that particular anxiety about human sexual relations and its dangers, it was correctly foreseen by many that the acceptance of birth control would lead to a different emphasis in sex and family life. Whereas some families before that date may have been stretched for resources initially, children, as they grew older, became an asset to a family. In agricultural societies, a large family could all work together for the maintenance of the whole farming enterprise. In many families, there were traditions of working in a particular industry, trade, or craft, and young people followed their parents' line of work. The care given to the children by their parents was reciprocated by the children's care of the older generation as the years passed, sanctified by the same tradition. It was both heartwarming and essential before the time of retirement planning—and one has to say that in our own time it is still important, Social Security and 401ks notwithstanding. Grandmothers often helped with child care. The children in their middle age saw to it that their parents were not left destitute or lonely. People are, in the phrase of the Jewish demographer Julian Simon, "the ultimate resource."[7] Incidentally, it is true by a seeming paradox, as we saw above, that one child is much harder to look after than three or four! When there are siblings, they relate to each other as well as to their parents, and that lifts a great load off the shoulders of the mother in particular. The children more or less bring each other up.

Before 1930, all Christian churches and denominations saw that the child was the God-given center of marriage. Just as God made us to need food for health and vigor and sleep for rest, so he gave us the yearning to love one another as sexual beings, so that within the sheltering love of the parents, a new person could come into the world continuing God's work of creation, to be loved by God and to love him in turn, while at the same time husband and wife could be knit together in a holistic way, their loving sexually expressed. In 1930, however, the Lambeth Conference of the Church of England decided that birth control, using the barrier methods available at the time, was permitted—though only to married couples. It was as if God wanted his purpose in giving couples this urge to love and power to come together to give life to another to be negated, not by self-mastery in the consideration of their circumstances, but by recourse to a barrier of thin latex! This decision pierced as if with a lance the unanimity of Christian denominations with the Catholic Church in the matter of sexual morality. It had consequences that must have been unforeseen by that conference at Lambeth. The proposition was flawed in essence and impossible in the limitation it imposed, as if any system could police the provision of contraceptives only to married couples.

Many voices dissented at the time. Even Sigmund Freud, the preeminent psychologist of the day and a man of no religious faith, recognized in birth control "the abandonment of the reproductive function," which he saw as the common feature of all perversions. "We actually describe a sexual activity as perverse if it has given up the aim of reproduction and pursues the attainment of pleasure as an aim independent of it."[8] Freud and many other distinguished people within and without the Christian tradition, including the Hindu Mahatma Ghandi, recognized that to refocus marriage on the achievement of sexual pleasure as its essential purpose (with the Christian understanding of the co-creation, with God, of children as essentially an optional extra) would be to knock the institution of marriage sideways. And they were right.

No one can deny that almost eighty years later, marriage is more often subject to breakdown or is sidestepped altogether, so that sexual partnerships are looser and more frequently thrown aside, often to the great distress of one or other of the couple—not to mention their children.

It has also resulted in a much greater sexualization of society, in which sexual pleasure, without the context of committed love, is paraded in a way that is almost obsessive. This is not only evidenced in works of art and performance, but even government has aligned itself with the trend by promoting sex education that appears to have little understanding of marriage as a serious sexual commitment; instead, it concentrates on giving advice on using condoms and proposing an equivalence between homosexual relationships and marriage.[9]

Seeing sexual satisfaction as the primary good of marriage instead of enjoying it as a wonderful part of the whole relationship clearly leads people to judge all sexual relationships by that same standard—whether between the sexes, between two members of the same sex, or anything else. Exclude the possibility of the baby, and every other fancy can be accommodated.

The Catholic Church has upheld her historic teaching, while many other Christian denominations have come to accept contraception and do not condemn killing in the womb, though many individual Christians oppose it. Some promoters of contraception specifically state that because no contraceptive is 100 percent effective at all times, abortion is a necessary backup. The absence of the child is paramount. As Malcom Potts, then the medical director of the Planned Parenthood Federation, said in a talk in Cambridge, England, "There is overwhelming evidence that, contrary to what you might expect, the availability of contraceptives leads to an increase in the abortion rate."[10]

Birth control is not a new thing. The early Christians lived in a society that accepted the methods of birth control then in existence: barriers of sorts and abortifacient potions, as well as direct abortions. Roman fathers would inspect their male babies to make sure they were free from deformity or weakness before deciding whether to let them live or not (Rome needed young men as soldiers). Girl babies did not have to be kept at all, and few Roman families kept more than one girl.[11] Now, much like the ancient Romans, except with the aid of our new technology, we have abortions if a child in the womb is thought to be likely to suffer some disablement, and this is permitted up to the time of birth, even for a minor defect that can be put right, such as a cleft palate. On January 25, 2004, the *Sunday Telegraph* reported that Professor John Harris, a member of the British Medical Association's ethics committee, said it was "not plausible to think that there is any moral change that occurs during the journey down the birth canal." Of course, that is absolutely correct. However, he is reported to have preceded that remark to the House of Commons Science and Technology Committee with the words, "I don't think infanticide is always unjustifiable." As a counselor, I have encountered an inquiry about the possibility of abortion if the preborn baby happened to be a girl. The early Christians rejected the pagan way, and through their Christian faith they saw the love and gift of God in the birth of their children and realized that each child had an immortal destiny.

The Church has always recognized that life begins at conception, as it evidently does. There are two separate elements, sperm and egg; when they fuse, a new human being comes into the world, within the womb of the mother—first one cell, then two, then four, and so on. Before the invention of the microscope in the seventeenth century, the actual process of conception was not known and some people thought that the soul, which they rightly saw as the spiritual element of personhood, came into the developing body at a later date. But as they were not certain about this, they still taught that the new life was sacred because it existed, even while in the womb.

Very recently, in the last twenty years, some doctors have claimed that life does not begin until implantation of the blastocyst (that is, the new being) in the lining of the mother's womb. These medical professionals do not concern themselves with the spirit, but by using the new definition of the beginning of human life, they seek to legitimize the use of human beings at the early embryo stage in research, as if they were not human beings. They also accept the procuring of early chemical abortions by means of the frivolous-sounding name of the "morning-after pill." This is a risk to the mother's health; its effects are painful and unpleasant and, if it does what the manufacturers claim it will do, it destroys a small life. Why it should be supposed that this new being is not human when its parents are human is not made plain. After all, there has to be a new entity to get itself into the welcoming lining of the mother's womb. What can that entity be, if it is not human? And to be human, a being consists of both body and spirit.

Many women have their babies aborted through fear—fear of boyfriends, husbands, parents, or a general fear of the future with a baby. No one can judge the guilt of others. Many who work in health care may associate the suppression of the most vulnerable with compassion for the mother, though it is a false compassion. To encourage conflict between a child newly conceived and the mother is, considered dispassionately, a terrible thing. Governments cynically permit it as a cheaper option than supporting the mother. One can only see it as a kind of war against the child. It is a fact that, in the law of many countries, human life is now disposable up to the time at which the baby could live outside the womb, and if there is a fear of disablement, even something minor and capable of being remedied, that life can be destroyed up to birth in the United Kingdom (except, thank God, in Northern Ireland). In the United States, historically, *Roe v. Wade* has allowed for late-term abortions if they are deemed necessary "for the preservation of the life or health of the mother" (*Roe,* 410 U.S., at 164–65), a statement that can be loosely interpreted. *Doe v. Bolton, Roe's* companion case, interpreted the "health of the mother" to encompass any factor contributing to the well-being of the mother, including physical, emotional, and psychological states, as well as familial factors and age. Currently, abortion continues to be a highly debated issue within the United States, and laws vary from state to state. The Church understands that the spiritual part of a human being, which being immaterial cannot be weighed or measured, coexists with the physical; it is impossible to separate the two, so at conception, spirit and body are both there, making up the new human being with an immortal soul and its own validity as a human person.

Difficulties for Married Couples in Our Society

It is very clear that our society makes it hard for couples to sustain the upbringing of a large family—unless they have well-above-average earning power. Housing is very expensive in many parts of the United States, except perhaps in those places where there is little available work. When mortgage lenders started to sell mortgages on the basis of two incomes instead of one, it meant that husbands and wives both had to work hard and continuously to pay for the roof over their heads—and, of course, it sent house prices up, which meant that couples had to work harder than ever to buy a home for themselves. It is often necessary and desirable to space pregnancies for the good of all, while keeping in the forefront of one's mind that children are at the heart of Christian marriage.

Natural Family Planning: the Natural Way to Space Children

The human body is a marvelous entity, a wonderfully intricate web of functions and capabilities designed by a master hand. It has the ability to grow, to mature, to sustain itself, before it slows down and gradually ages. In its sexual functions, too, we find the same precision of creation—the testes growing outside the male body, because they need to be colder than the rest of the body to function properly; the female sexual organs growing within the body, because they need greater warmth than the rest of the body. The facts of the female cycle of fertility reveal the same order and precision in a healthy woman. The divine Maker of all this did not leave spouses with an impossible conundrum if, having thought about it seriously, husband and wife together decide that they need to postpone another pregnancy or that their family is complete.

We sometimes look back and regret that medical science had not advanced further in times past, so that, for instance, Mozart could have lived longer or Beethoven's deafness could have been cured. Not, of course, that a woman's cycle of fertility is akin to illness—far from it. But it did require the skill of doctors to map it and understand its course. If only research had discovered before the last eighty years or so the delicate mechanism of the woman's procreative cycle, then perhaps the destructive rush to contraception and abortion might have had less impact!

We begin with the sperm: in each ejaculation, there are said to be between two and five hundred million sperm—and yet only one sperm is required to fertilize the egg, which is one of the thousands with which each little girl is endowed at the beginning of her life. Egg and sperm each contribute 50 percent of the new human being's hereditary material, despite the fact that the egg is about ninety thousand times the size of the sperm.[12] As she grows up, a girl's body enters into the cycle of fertility, which lasts until late middle age. Each month, at one point in the girl's and then woman's cycle, a hormone known as the "follicle stimulating hormone" is released into the bloodstream, and an egg matures. While this is taking place, the amount of this hormone decreases to ensure that only one egg, or occasionally two, is released in one cycle. Next, the lining of the womb (the uterus) starts to thicken in order to be ready to receive the egg if it is fertilized. The egg is released into the Fallopian tube, and this is known as ovulation. At the same time, mucus is produced in the cervix. In the course of a cycle, two different kinds of mucus are produced there. The first type can be observed externally; it starts as sticky and cloudy and then becomes very stretchy and clear. It can also feel lubricative when one wipes. During the fertile time, this mucus forms something like tubes, which allow the sperm to swim up and reach the egg in order to fertilize it. The second sort of mucus is not visible externally, as it is thick and dense and acts like a plug, so that it forms a barrier to the entry of the sperm from ovulation to menstruation. This is to ensure that only one egg, or occasionally two, is released in one cycle, and therefore can be fertilized in one cycle, and only on one day. If a second ovulation occurs, it can only be in the same twenty-four hours. A woman checks her "observable mucus days" and "dry days" simply by wiping and observing, and this needs to be done on a daily basis. Up to the point of ovulation, the signs of fertility have to be looked for especially carefully, so that any "observable mucus days" are not missed. If no conception takes place during the cycle, the lining of the womb cleans itself out ("menstruation"), and the process begins all over again.

It is important to check every day, in order to be aware of what the body is doing. All observations have to be noted down on a chart, often by simply sticking special stamps to it. This may sound like a chore, but it soon becomes second nature. According to the Creighton Model, keeping the chart is the husband's job! The part he plays in the business of fertility management is essential. His cooperation is integral to the Creighton Model and all other models, such as the Billings Method and the Sympto-Thermal, of which I am aware. Both Billings and the Sympto-Thermal are also based on mucus observation, and the latter adds observation of early morning temperature levels. The latter two methods take into account that some women may prefer to keep their own charts, or notes, but keep their husband up-to-date. It is, however, always a matter for both husband and wife (not for the wife alone). Therefore, if for a serious reason a couple want to avoid conceiving another child, they can learn to pinpoint the true time of fertility and agree to wait for the infertile time, postponing intercourse and all genital touching. The next question is, how long does that take?

As we saw above, when the woman has ovulated, the egg survives not more than twenty-four hours. The sperm, however, can live in the woman's body for some five days, but they need mucus to survive so long. In the post-ovulatory phase of the woman's cycle, fertilization cannot occur because there is normally no egg. If there were an egg, the thick mucus would prevent the sperm from reaching it; the full-time use of barriers, chemical contraception, and still more long-term implants is taking a huge hammer to crush an egg.

There are also other indicators during the cycle, such as a rise in the body temperature at ovulation, which is maintained during the post-ovulation phase, and by changes in the cervix, both in its position relative to the vagina and in a change in its texture (it feels softer). The cervical os (that is, the "mouth" or orifice) opens, which indicates the opening up of the uterus.

In order to make sure that no pregnancy occurs, couples need to abstain from intercourse for an average of six to eight days according to the Creighton Model, and a little longer according to other models, when mucus is observed. It is important to state that couples need to be instructed in how to observe the changes by a properly trained teacher. It is not difficult and does not take long to learn. It has been taught, very successfully, by Mother Teresa's sisters in the poorest parts of Calcutta. And the husband-and-wife team of the Drs. Billings, from Australia, who first established the mucus differentials as a way of discerning the fertile time, have taught the method successfully in some parts of China at the invitation of the Chinese government; there are now as many as 37 thousand trained fertility management teachers there.

Of course, it would be pleasant to be able to be without restrictions of any sort, but as means of avoiding conception, barriers and chemicals also have real and in some cases very serious drawbacks, in addition to negating the essence of that openness to the other that is at the heart of marriage. To know the reason for a time of abstaining gives a sense of self-mastery. It is also possible and rewarding to be able to use the time to express affection without sex and to look forward with a sense of excitement to the end of the time of abstinence.

In this way, and without separating the loving, uniting act from the procreative, couples are using the natural cycle to achieve their necessary goal. They are using the God-given variables for a good reason. This is quite different in kind from using contraceptives—even though, in each case, the couple do not want a pregnancy at that time. Contraceptives cut across the natu-

ral order; natural fertility management goes with it. That is why
the Church forbids the use of contraceptives while accepting use
of the natural cycles of the body—God-given in themselves. The
two ends or purposes of sex, the loving and the procreative, are
so closely knit that the Church has always taught that to divide
them is to negate their two-in-oneness, their essential nature.

If a couple learn to observe carefully and abstain from intercourse and genital touching for the fertile time, the method is
99.5 percent effective in avoiding pregnancy.[13] It makes use of
the body's own program, so no barriers are put between the
spouses, and there are no harmful side effects. It also encourages
the couple to communicate their intimate concerns and thus
brings mutual closeness. The woman comes to "center" herself in
her own body, becoming increasingly aware of it and its rhythms
as a life-giving force.

It has also been observed time and time again that couples
using natural methods of spacing their family achieve an intimate
sense of a shared plan, which is quite different from couples in
which one partner or the other is responsible for making sure
that no baby is conceived. Incidence of divorce is significantly
lower as well (approximately 1 percent of couples). Using barrier
methods in times of fertility negates the proper benefits of this
method of mutual support and undermines the couple's understanding of what they are doing; it is this understanding that
deepens their perception of marriage. The instructor of fertility
management really needs to share an appreciation of the method,
not just the technique, because it involves the whole relationship.
There is a matter for wonder in the intricate and delicate way a
woman's body prepares for a child to be conceived and awaits the
sperm that will join with her egg for the wonderful outcome of
the birth of the son or daughter. By managing their fertility, the
couple retain their awareness of it. The Creighton Model System
looks to the spiritual, physical, intellectual, creative, and emotional elements in the life of the woman—SPICE for short. All

teachers using the discoveries of the Drs. Billings have similar concerns.

In all but the last century or so, no one, to my knowledge, questioned that the sexual act was properly and inherently both creative and loving, though many people failed in practice to live in true love. The whole Judeo-Christian tradition accepted children as a rich gift—although in individual cases they may not have been welcomed. Recently, individuals (and other Christian denominations) have suggested that the creation of children is less important than the happiness of husband and wife, and that children should be, more or less, forcibly kept at bay by the barriers that keep husband and wife apart, which are to be removed perhaps once in a marriage. It is noticeable that these ideas have been developed primarily in the affluent Western world, where having more children is often seen as precluding the getting of more things. In less materialistic societies, children are still welcomed (to the fury of many governments).

Infertility and Heartache

So much effort nowadays is put into avoiding pregnancy that many couples are dismayed to find when they hope for a child that they do not conceive quickly. Women are at their most fertile in their teens and twenties, and many women at the present time do not marry young. There are many causes of infertility, and the heartache accompanying it is very real and sometimes devastating. However, there is much help to be found in a proper understanding of human reproduction and its problems.

A Billings Method teacher can help here. The couple can be taught to understand the subtle changes in the mucus secretion or sensation, alerting them to the most fertile time in the cycle. NaProTechnology is a "recently developed reproductive science" that comprises the medical applications that go hand-in-hand with the Creighton Model System (of charting the cyclical changes) and is of use in overcoming infertility. In 40–60 percent of couples undergoing treatment with NaPro, a pregnancy is achieved. Each treatment is individually planned; if hormonal treatment is indicated, natural hormones are used, and all processes are body-friendly.

By contrast, couples with fertility problems are often urged to go for *in vitro* fertilization (IVF). *In vitro* simply means "in a glass dish." This technique involves stimulating the woman's ovaries, causing the woman to super-ovulate so that there are more eggs for fertilization. The eggs are then put into the dish with sperm, and if they are fertilized, the new human beings are scanned for any possible malformation or weakness. Only the best one or two of these human beings at this early stage of their development are chosen, and the rest are destroyed. There is a choice of freezing some for later use, yet these are not vegetables. What other innocent human beings do we destroy, except, by a terrible irony, those in our "fertility" clinics and hospitals?

The preparation of the woman for this process and the internal investigations are often painful and distressing. The success rate varies from clinic to clinic but is not particularly high. Treatment is very expensive. The Centers for Disease Control and Prevention put the average figure around 33 percent for live births occurring after such treatment, although the figure drops drastically for older patients. There is also a higher rate of serious abnormalities in those children conceived by this method, and many die through miscarriage or abortion after they are implanted in the mother's womb, including those who have been frozen. Relatively few are brought to birth.

With *in vitro* fertilization, the most intimate of all human acts is handed over to a technician, because the couple want a child so much. Much has to be left to the discretion of those running the clinic. A case came to light where it was obvious that there had been a mix-up in the fertilization process, because the twin children were black and the mother and the supposed father were white.[14] Another case was brought to court when a boy noticed that he did not at all resemble his supposed father. The boy felt an urgent need to know who he was and who his father was. The latter was instructed by the Family Division of the High Court (U.K.) to take a DNA test, which did, indeed, reveal that he was not the father.[15] By this time he was divorced from the mother of the boy. It seems unlikely that these are the only incidents of confusion in the process.

Fortunately, even a simple knowledge of a woman's cycle of fertility can, in some cases, help the couple to find the right time to conceive. Beyond that, Natural Procreative Technology can assist by ameliorating many conditions in a body-friendly way and with a higher success rate than that of IVF. This is the way forward for anyone, whatever their beliefs. But it derives from the vision of God's purposes, which he sets forth in the very personhood of man and woman.

The manufacture and sale of condoms, contraceptive pills, and even the less popular intrauterine devices and implants are all very big business, a multimillion dollar industry, with worldwide distribution. It is therefore likely in business terms that the manufacturers will seek to cast doubt on natural methods in order to protect their investment and livelihood. Teachers and proponents of the latter have to eat, like everyone else, but they have a vision of their work beyond financial profits. Some of them have expressed to me their excitement and level of commitment to this revelation of God's overarching, creative love, which is indeed a true theology of the body.

Unfortunately, some couples do not conceive even after treatment. This can be a matter of great sadness. Adoption is, of course, a good possibility, though there are few young babies available for adoption at this time.[16] It seems very hard and unfair that some people cannot have children, and in their disappointment they deserve much love, many prayers, and real sympathetic understanding. Teachers of fertility management will still be a support.

The love of the couple for each other will be of the greatest help to them. That love will fill them in turn with the love of others and the growth of their love for God and his saints, who will become more vividly their heavenly family.

See the Appendix for a list of Natural Family Planning centers.

For Further Exploration

1. A couple wishing to marry in a Catholic Church have to answer three questions in the affirmative. The third is: "Are you ready to accept children lovingly from God and bring them up according to the law of Christ and his Church?" Does this refer to the acceptance of children in the womb? Are there other circumstances to which it could be relevant?

2. In Catholic teaching, conceiving a child is sharing in God's loving creation. What implications does this have for parents?

3. What are the advantages of *Natural Family Planning?* How does it bring the couple closer together?

REFLECTION

"I love you, you're perfect, now change!" If someone you love seems to put conditions on loving, what effect can that have on the relationship? Consider the impact that contraception has had on society in the Western world in the last eighty years. As far as we can tell, are there more happy marriages now than there were? Are there more broken marriages? Has contraception done away with "unwanted children"?

CHAPTER 6

New Life, New Excitement

The test is positive: the baby has arrived! Arrived already? Arrived where? The mother's body is in a ferment of excitement; one sperm has won the race; the egg-of-the-month has been fertilized; she is pregnant, she is with child, and this new human being has taken up residence in his or her very first home—the mother's body! The new baby depends utterly on the mother. No wonder that as soon as babies can feel anything, they feel love for their mothers. All the same, babies are separate human beings from conception onward; they need their mothers to provide food, shelter, and protection, but they are not organs of their mothers' bodies. New babies may have different blood types from their mothers. And new mothers know soon enough that their babies have lives of their own when the kicking begins!

Millions of the new mother's husband's tiny sperms have competed for this one egg; one of them has penetrated the outer covering and moved inwards to the nucleus.[1] The head of the sperm and the nucleus of the egg combined their contents to form a new individual. Each contributes half of the new human being's inherited characteristics. Yet the mix of these characteristics is unique; no two are ever identical.[2] The single fertilized egg instantly divides to form two cells, then four, and so on. Some of the cells become protective tissues; some form the embryo, the early stage of being a baby.

In St. Luke's Gospel, we enter the enchanting scene when our Lady, Mary, carrying in her womb the newly and supernaturally conceived Son of God, goes to visit and help her much older cousin. Elizabeth's own baby (also miraculous, though in a different sense, because she was old and she and her husband had long been childless), the future John the Baptist, is about six months old in the womb. When Mary enters Elizabeth's house, Elizabeth's baby leaps for joy in her womb, sensing in some way that Jesus, Emmanuel, which means "God with us," is present. Elizabeth herself welcomes Mary as "the mother of my Lord," something that she had learned directly through the Holy Spirit. The Gospel reads: "*As soon* as Elizabeth heard Mary's greeting the child leapt in her womb and Elizabeth was filled with the Holy Spirit."[3] According to the Gospel, therefore, Mary had not had time to tell her cousin her amazing news. Do babies leap for joy? Well, a new technique of ultrasound pictures shows us a baby in the womb smiling at twenty-six weeks after conception![4] The same ultrasound shows babies moving their limbs at eight weeks after conception, moving their fingers at fifteen weeks, and yawning (already!) at twenty weeks. They certainly kick and jump and do somersaults, comfortable in their water bubble. They practice sucking on their thumbs. They can also be seen crying, and they are known to feel pain; in short, they are human.

At the point when her pregnancy is confirmed, the mother may feel a turmoil in her emotions. She welcomes the baby for which she and her husband have longed, and yet she may have other emotions simultaneously: fear, loss of control, worry about how she and her husband will be able to cope with this very new situation. Our bodies, part of God's good creation, being part of what it is to be human, can affect our emotions and our thinking. At the early stages of pregnancy, the changes taking place in a woman can take their toll. There are hormonal changes, and her body has to work harder than usual to accommodate the new life within her, so she is likely to feel more tired. With the best will in the world, she may still find herself tearful and depressed. The best thing she can do is to tell herself the truth, which is that these feelings will almost certainly pass as the pregnancy progresses and that any discomfort and uncertainty are part of this great project: the birth and raising of another child of God.

She will also anxiously watch her husband's emotions. He will almost certainly feel great pride in his wife (and in himself). But he may also feel worried at the implications of what they have taken on. He may simply be too cheerful for her taste about the whole enterprise, accepting too easily the fact that she will be giving birth; however attuned and sympathetic he may be, *he* won't be giving birth! Or he may feel fearful of the responsibilities that will be his along with hers. He may fear that his place in his wife's affections will be usurped. Both spouses must strive to remain aware of the other's anxieties and accept the other's fears. It is very difficult to be open without the security of knowing that the other person will understand—or at least accept. It may be a relief to know that these feelings are not uncommon. It is less a matter of questioning each other and more a matter of elucidating the other's feelings. In this way, both will be able to reassure each other. Whatever their feelings, the couple have this wondrous occurrence to thank God for, as he is the source of life. Through the conception of their baby, God has allowed them to join him in the work of creation, to become co-creators with him. This is where the Christian view enables parents to see that their already loved baby is not just a charming little toy to be kissed and bought presents, but a human being in relationship with the three Persons of the Trinity. Like marriage, the birth of their baby is not simply a private matter but a great and wonderful interaction between heaven and earth.

It is right for the mother to feel special at this time. Although she is not ill, she should cosset herself, within reason. She must eat the right food and give herself the chance to rest when she can. She need not pretend that having a baby is just something you can do as an optional extra to your usual lifestyle. She can continue her work and play, with just that bit of added care. A film star in the 1960s, announcing her pregnancy, was quoted as saying, "Having a baby is just six weeks off work for a girl nowadays." I imagine the experience of giving birth taught her differently.

A pregnancy is always measured from the date of the last menstruation, because that date can be ascertained, but it seems rather a cheat and makes the pregnancy seem longer than it is. Nine months may seem a long time for the parents, but considering how much has to take place, it is amazing that it takes only nine months. First, the baby has to tuck him- or herself into the nest that is the lining of the mother's womb, where the placenta will form—partly from the baby's tissues and partly from the mother's. Through the placenta, nourishment will be passed from the mother's blood circulation and the new baby's cord.

The heart, a potent symbol of living individuality, starts beating at about twenty-one days after conception. By about six weeks after conception, the baby has all his or her organs in place. Now they only have to develop. At the same stage, the brain and the nervous system are beginning to function, and bones start to take over from the cartilage of the early weeks. Doctors now call the baby a "fetus," which just means "little one" in Latin. He or she is an embryo no longer and, in any case, whether embryo or fetus, he or she is a human being, a person from the start.

At about the same time, the mother sometimes starts to feel sick in the mornings or during the entire day. This does not usually last long, but it may be caused by the different hormones in her body at this time, which may also cause additional tiredness. At this stage, when the baby's limbs are developing, it is well to keep away from any medication unless the mother's regular doctor positively recommends it, because, as was so tragically discovered with thalidomide, developing limbs can be affected by certain chemicals that may be part of the makeup of the medication.

Once the stage of sickness has passed, usually by the end of the first three months of the baby's life, the mother will probably feel very well. Her skin always looks good at this stage of pregnancy, and she will soon start to show. She should, however, continue to be careful about any drugs or treatment, which can still affect the baby's growth. She and her husband should consider very careful-ly any suggestion from the hospital staff about further tests recom-mended for any reason. Unhappily, there are still few treatments that can be applied to babies in the womb. So tests are often a pre-lude to a recommendation to abort the baby if there is any possi-bility of disablement. Diagnosis of disability is not exact with a preborn baby, and a geneticist from Oxford was quoted recently as saying that "some anomaly seen on a fetal scan is all too often simply a normal variation."[5] After all, we are individual and differ-ent from each other. To suggest that such a reading reveals with certainty that something is wrong can be misleading, and in some cases, the intrusive testing procedures risk harm to the baby. There is no requirement to have these suggested tests.

The middle three months of a pregnancy are usually a happy time, because the mother feels well and is blooming. The baby's presence is felt more and more each day, and the excitement of the first kick that the mother notices is tremendous. At this stage, it feels like a tickle with a feather! The baby still has the room to move about (by the end, the baby will be limited in his or her movements by lack of space) and at sixteen weeks' old is all of five and half inches long in a sitting position, from head to bottom! The baby is growing bigger at a great rate, and the mother, however well and energetic she feels, should make sure that she gets extra rest. A lot is still happening in her body, and she needs to be aware of the baby's demands on her.

Home or Hospital for the Birth?

The idea of giving birth in your own home may be attrac-tive. Staying cozily in one's own nest, with one's husband and the midwife, perhaps a birthing pool and maybe one's mother near-by, sounds like the perfect environment for the baby to be born into. However, certain questions need to be considered. Is the midwifery team big enough to give the sort of care that is necessary and reassuring? How far is home from the nearest hospital maternity unit, in case of an emergency?

Nobody likes hospitals, but they are prepared for bringing babies into the world and are able to provide caesarian sections, should this be necessary. Perhaps a first baby needs the additional care of a hospital, but if that birth is worry-free then later babies can be born safely at home.

Many first-time mothers are very idealistic and want their baby's birth to be without medical intervention, even pain relief. Giving birth is a very energetic thing to do, and many mothers will, in practice, be glad of something that can help them on their way. Pain can be relieved at each stage, and although heavy sedation can slow the baby down, relief can be given in a way that does not add to the baby's trauma.

Should the Father Be Present?

Although for centuries giving birth was considered an event that only women should witness, it does seem unfair that the father should miss the wonderful moment of his child's appearance in the world. He can be a prop, literally and spiritually, to his wife. He will see her efforts on behalf of their child and be grateful as well as delighted.

On the other hand, his wife may be too absorbed in the process of giving birth, and the husband may feel ignored while midwives and nurses concentrate on the drama. The mother may simply want to get on with the job at hand with the professionals in attendance, and then have the pleasure afterward of showing their baby, clean and well wrapped up, to his or her father. I think this is an occasion when the mother's preference should be consulted. She has a lot to deal with in giving birth.

Even then, when the baby has safely arrived, his mother may at first feel too tired to enter into the general rejoicing. But very soon she and her husband will feel amazement at the tiny, noisy bundle that is their daughter or son. That is the moment to thank God, together.

Two into Three!

If marriage is the most cataclysmic event up to that point in the life of a couple, the fruit of their marriage, their first child, is the author of an even greater upheaval! This tiny living entity rules the roost, destroys peace and quiet, ruins sleep, creates endless washing, costs a fortune in equipment and necessities, and yet is wonderful, the most remarkable baby of all babies and the amazement of family and friends![6]

To be a baby, as we all were once, is to have arrived in the outside world in a sort of Alice-in-Wonderland way. We are aware of the mother's trauma during the birth of her child, but what about the trauma of the child? From a warm, wet, comfortable existence in the gentle dark, hearing his or her mother's steady heartbeat and her voice, the baby comes out with a rush, pushed in most cases by the mother's strenuous efforts, into a world that is much colder than the womb and is full of what must seem like blinding light. The baby has not had to breathe for him or herself in the womb; oxygen came through the blood of the umbilical cord. But now a new baby has to learn how to do it for him- or herself, taking in the oxygen from the air, inflating his or her little lungs, and getting rid of the mucus that will still be there and in the eyes and ears. A loud cry is the way forward, and a sharpish pat on the back by the midwife or doctor often helps.

Now the heart has to start its individual working, separating the fresh blood from the used blood by way of the valve in the heart, and waste matter is excreted by the new baby and not, as during life in the womb, through the mother's body. The linking cord is cut soon after birth, and a special jelly within the cord expands when the cord is cut to plug the cut and stop the bleeding; otherwise, the baby could lose too much blood. One cannot help saying with the psalmist:

> I praise you, for I am fearfully and wonderfully made.
> Wonderful are your works;
> that I know very well. (Ps 139:14)

The Lord seems to have thought of everything!

Finally, the afterbirth, or placenta, comes away; "it is an extraordinary organ, one of the most potent and versatile nature ever devised."[7] The placenta has done everything for the baby in the womb: through the umbilical cord, it has nourished the baby, removed waste matter, and protected him or her from things that might be harmful. The umbilical cord contains two separate "vessels," one to the mother, the other to the baby; but though they are separate, their walls are permeable and permit an exchange of products between mother and child. Because the child is separate from the mother, the mother's body would reject the child at the embryo stage as, literally, a "foreign body" if their circulatory systems were directly connected.

Of course, the baby cannot consciously take responsibility for anything; her incapability is complete. Yet she is ready for the slow ascent into consciousness and can already make her needs known. It is not only the mother who feels tired after the birth; it is the baby, too.

How to Feed?

The mother's milk does not come until the third day after the birth of her baby. The baby can still be put to the breast because, before the arrival of the milk, the mother's breasts have a thick substance called colostrum that starts the baby off with nursing.

Everyone now agrees that a mother's milk is best for the baby. It contains everything a baby needs and in addition immunizes him from various illnesses for the first months. Breast-feeding also combines feeding and hugging, because the way the baby is held to the breast gives a real feeling of closeness, which is as enjoyable to the mother as it is to the little one. The midwife's or breast-feeding counselor's help in teaching the best position for holding the baby (there are more technical tricks than one might suppose) will be invaluable. Bottle-feeding can be impersonal. However, an occasional bottle in an emergency does not hurt the baby and may be a lifesaver for the mother. If she wants, she can, of course, express her milk and leave it in a bottle in the fridge.

The initial few days of nursing can be traumatic. Until the woman's nipples harden, they can be very sensitive, and the mother should seek help if the discomfort is severe or does not get better, as there may be a problem such as thrush or even mastitis. Breast shields, which cover the nipples, can be useful. But unless the mother really cannot bear the discomfort when she starts nursing, or finds the very idea of nursing distasteful, it is in the interests of both baby and mother to continue. Breast milk is there ready even at night, it is cheap, it is the right stuff for the new person, and, as they say, the cat can't get it.

Though the mother is almost inevitably the primary carer and feeder, the father can do a great deal to ensure that his wife does not feel that everything is up to her. Contemporary husbands, in my experience, are very good at changing diapers, bathing, and entertaining—all of which are very important. The baby will like it, too, relishing a bit of variety in being looked after.

Sleeping Patterns

This is not a book about how to bring up children. There are many available, and I much enjoyed Lynette Burrow's book, *Good Children*. With her family of six, she is full of practical and cheerful suggestions.[8]

On the new baby's sleeping arrangements, she strongly recommends keeping the baby in the busiest room, the one where most family activities go on, and in the parents' room at night. She points out that the world of the womb is not a silent one; the baby hears gurglings from the mother's stomach and the pumping of blood as well as the mother's heartbeat and the sound of her voice. So a silent nursery may well seem stranger to the baby than a place where the parents are chatting and the radio or TV is blaring away; he or she may fall asleep more readily where the living is going on. Babies, Burrow maintains, do not mind noise, unless it is very sudden. This is a brave view, but it is also probably the way things used to be. Lynette Burrows points out that old pictures of cottage interiors always show the cradle in the kitchen—for one thing, it was warm.

Some mothers may prefer the baby to be in a quiet room when he or she sleeps during the day and, after a few months, at night as well. It gives the parents some time to themselves, and when the baby reaches toddler stage, they are spared the business of overtired children, reluctant to let go, hanging around the adult dinner table and inhibiting, or rather hindering, relaxing conversation. In the end, every mother and father will decide for themselves what works best for them and the baby.

Tiredness is likely to be a dominant concern for the mother in the first weeks after the birth. Here the husband can do a great deal by way of supporting her, encouraging her to sleep when the baby does, and understanding her exhaustion. He may be feeling pretty tired himself, what with emotion and interrupted nights, even if his wife does the feeding, but she has played the major role in the drama. A spare room, or even the living room sofa (if big enough), can be very useful to enable the father to get enough sleep to earn the next day's meal.

However, the wonder of this new person is overwhelming, and to feel his little body against one's shoulder or her head against the breast is to experience love in a unique way—parents, grandparents, even friends feel this. Glory be to God for little ones!

Baby Blues

Some new parents, both mothers and fathers, find the challenges of their baby almost overwhelming and can find themselves depressed—what the magazines call "Baby Blues." Many different perceptions and feelings can cause it, physical and emotional. Physical difficulties are a matter for medical investigation, and the tiredness that is almost endemic with a new baby must be taken seriously. Depression may hit the father as well as the mother, and as he is likely, at least after the first week or so, to be doing his usual job, he may find himself under a strain he perhaps had not anticipated. He may also feel jealous that his loving wife now seems more interested in the baby (his baby!) than in him. This is a difficult time for both.

According to Jane Feinmann in her book *Baby Blues,*[9] two suggestions work in dealing with these troubles. One is the role of the health visitor, who ideally should be able to spend time with the mother both before and after the birth, so that she can frankly discuss the things that are worrying her. It is true that there is a great advantage in being able to talk freely to someone outside the family in whom one has confidence. Sometimes, with family and friends the mother may not want to admit her feelings, seeing them as an admission of weakness or the beginning of failure.

The other suggestion concerns the parents and their feelings about each other in the context of new parenthood. Feinmann strongly recommends a great deal of talking together and expressing to each other any worries they have and any distress they feel. Touching is important here. Hands or arms entwined provide the link that words may not, at this time, be expressing. They may also find it difficult to regain their usual expression of love through sex. Mel Parr proposes that if the mother loses interest at this time, it may be a "biological restraint" left over from primitive times, when a baby required its mother's full attention to survive. Talking about the conflicting roles of mother and lover, she suggests, can be enlightening.[10] A brief prayer through the exhaustion will also help.

Father and mother may both begin to worry about fertility, not wanting the mother to conceive again immediately. A woman who is fully breast-feeding is infertile for fifty-six days. If she is bottle-feeding, wholly or partially, she is infertile for twenty-seven days. Her periods may not return for up to eighteen months, and she can ovulate before her first period, but she can still chart her mucus and thus see when she is ovulating.

Wives have usually been working before the arrival of the baby, so they will have been contributing to the family purse and may have had their own bank account. Depending on circumstances, this may change, at least for a time, while the new mother stays at home with the baby, and again adjustments have to be made to accommodate the new situation. It is probably best to talk freely about these with as much goodwill as possible, because the baby belongs to both parents.

Talking with Baby

Jane Feinmann speaks of research showing that mothers and babies communicate with each other by looking and talking (the baby "talks" by making noises or mouthing silently). By two months after birth, mother and baby can have a "conversation," each taking turns to say something. If a mother is depressed, she may look at her baby with a blank expression and not talk, and the baby may look away. The writer quotes studies that show that the baby imitates his or her mother's facial expressions and may well experience, in some way, what she is feeling. So if the mother is smiling, the baby flashes a little smile and feels content. If the mother's facial expression is blank or sad, it may similarly affect the baby. Feinmann even suggests that the baby may try to cheer the mother up with gurgles and little smiles!

Given the fact that psychology is not an exact science, it is not surprising that others have questioned the validity of this research, and some believe that short-term depression does not affect the baby significantly. It seems to me that it is probably useful to have some insight into the fact that a very small baby can communicate with his or her mother (and father, too), because the knowledge becomes a tool for helping the baby that even an exhausted mother or father can use.

It does sometimes happen that simulating an emotion—happiness, courage, or even interest—does actually promote that emotion, so that if we try to look cheerful, we find ourselves feeling cheerful (or at least more cheerful). If one's aim is to cheer the baby and it is successful in that the baby smiles or gurgles, the mood of the person doing the cheering lifts, too.

In her book, Feinmann gives a case history of a mother in the country without a car, who felt overwhelmed by caring for her two little ones, by the work of the house, and perhaps above all by her isolation. After many days spent crying while her husband was at work, days in which she was barely able to respond to the children, she finally telephoned a health care worker, who came and talked to her for two hours. Talking was a help, and the health care worker arranged an appointment for her with her doctor, who diagnosed her as suffering from "postpartum depression"—something she had never heard of before. She found it a relief to know that it was a recognized condition, not just some individual pathology of her own, beyond the reach of medicine. The doctor prescribed antidepressants for her. She had been taking the contraceptive pill, which is known to depress women, and felt better when she stopped taking it. Within a few weeks, she felt able to carry on, and "gradually life has gotten better." She described how creative things helped her: sewing, painting, and writing verses. She also found that talking to her husband was now possible, and volunteers from an organization that supports families called on her most weeks. Hers was a very severe case to which her own particular personal circumstances contributed. It is certainly a great help to a young mother to have family and friends, especially young mothers like herself, with whom she can swap anecdotes about baby symptoms and behavior to the satisfaction of all parties. A mother and toddler group in the parish or the neighborhood can be invaluable.

The same writer also points out that the parents' priority should not be to get everything right, as if there were only one way of looking after a baby and they had to pass an examination. It does not matter if washing up is left to a convenient time, if the mother is in her nightgown until midmorning, or if the ironing basket seems to grow items like weeds. A routine will ultimately be established, and by the time the baby is three months old, both mother and father, and even the baby him- or herself, will have achieved a sort of rhythm for each day. (The father's part being confined to the time when he is at home, of course!) Fortunately, there is no fear that the husband and wife will be some sort of paragons of parenthood. They will muddle through as cheerfully as they can. There is an old story of a tramp describing his clothes as a series of holes tied together with string. Parenthood is a series of compromises tied together with love.

The baby can be presumed not to have much idea of the future in the early months of his or her life after birth, and it may help the mother to fall into an understanding of life as here and now. During her pregnancy she would have been eagerly counting the weeks, but the arrival of the baby will help her relax to an appreciation of this special time as one without specific limits.

Paradoxically, a structure to the baby's day will eventually, after perhaps three months, provide a useful framework for everyone. A regular bedtime, with toys in bed and a story from six months or so—babies love looking at bright-colored pictures, though their attention span is short—times for breakfast and midmorning snooze, lunch and walk in the park, a rest at least in the first year, play, bath, and bed again, break up the day nicely, but of course there is no point in refusing to admit variations in the schedule because friends or family visit, the weather is nice, or the baby has ideas of his or her own about settling for a sleep. There is, however, no need to entertain if one does not feel up to it, and it may be a good idea not to plan too many things ahead. Anything that is planned brings obligations, and one more obligation may just be too many. On the other hand, casual contacts, especially with other young mothers, can be cheering and helpful, because most mothers have experienced similar troubles. Your church will also be a good point of contact. It is easy to chat with other mothers when they have been to Mass as well.

Parents cannot always provide everything they would like to give their baby. After the twelve weeks of statutory maternity leave, many mothers, however much they would like to stay at home longer with their little one, have to return to outside-the-home work. If they can manage to work part time, so much the better. If not, father and mother will want to look carefully at the day care that is available. The ratio of staff to children is one of the most important considerations. They need not feel guilty at leaving their baby if they need to do so.

Fathers and mothers have much to share here. Both will be experiencing extra demands along with pride and excitement in their new baby, and they will have to be sensitive to how the other person is feeling. Both need opportunities for rest, and the mother in particular needs time to recover from the drama of giving birth and its physical demands. Her husband needs to be aware of this.

There is also a category of persons called grandparents! Most grandparents like to be asked to help; they like to be appreciated, but they are often very ready to lend a hand, and the relationship that grows between them and their grandchildren is a valuable one for all concerned. New parents should not be shy about asking their parents or in-laws to babysit or take the baby for a walk, if they live fairly near. Grandmothers and grandfathers are proud of the next generation and know that they will miss a great deal of fun and interest by being standoffish. I expect St. Anne, Mary's mother, helped out with baby Jesus!

The baby is the center of a welter of emotions, of highs and lows, of delight and amusement, of exhaustion and sometimes gloom. Who said family life was dull? It involves the greatest possible drama in countless scenes. But everything passes. Sleepless nights with babies give way to toddlers getting into everything; toddlers become schoolchildren, proud of their new status. Adolescents appear and prefer not to get up until lunchtime and go to bed at dawn. Finally, sensible adults emerge—and the whole cycle starts up again with them! Thank God for families!

For Further Exploration

1. The coming of the baby brings so many changes. What steps do you think the new parents should take to keep their relationship in balance?

2. Babies are wonderful. Can you imagine the different feelings of love, excitement, and, perhaps, some anxiety that the parents might feel initially? What are some of the resources that might help a new parent through feelings of anxiety, exhaustion, or even depression? Write a prayer that a parent in this situation might offer to God.

REFLECTION

Think about the excitement and responsibilities that come with bringing a new human being into the world. Each baby has an immortal destiny. How does that affect his or her parents and their plans for him or her?

CHAPTER 7

The Domestic Church

"Christ chose to be born and grow up in the bosom of the holy family of Joseph and Mary. The Church is nothing other than the family of God." In its very earliest days, after Pentecost, it consisted of families who had become believers "together with all [their] households."[1]

Pope John Paul II speaks of love as the "fundamental and innate vocation of every human being."[2] He says that the first task of a family is to "live with fidelity the reality of communion in a constant effort to develop an authentic community of persons."[3] By this he means that husband and wife will need to open themselves each to the other in a continuous process in order to build that most fascinating of edifices, a family. The first "communion" is that of the husband and wife, because they are "no longer two, but one flesh";[4] they have left their parents to form their own family and are called, says John Paul II, to a total mutual giving.[5] This union spreads out into wider and wider circles, like a stone thrown into a pond, embracing children, brothers and sisters, and perhaps elderly parents or other relatives, natural or adoptive. The spouses have left their parents, but they receive them again, so to speak, in their new home. The family is both natural and supernatural, and the natural affections are enhanced and deepened by grace. This is what the document of Vatican II names "the domestic sanctuary of the Church."[6]

At first this concept may seem—well, churchy, pietistic, and rather off-putting. But I think that in so naming it, the Council and later Pope John Paul II are pointing the Church toward the family, not primarily bringing the family into the Church. After all, there are and always have been families who know nothing of Christ and his Church. The bonding and the babies have always been part of God's plan for humanity, and they are brought to a richer understanding of love by God's grace. A family is itself, and the Church is also a family, so that husband and wife, and later their children and others, draw into their relationships this universal family instituted by Christ himself. The Church is the guardian of the teachings of Christ, the dispenser of grace through the sacraments, and she is also the people who pray, who are able to call themselves the People of God. A church is a place where we raise our hearts and minds to him, where he comes to us, hidden in what looks and tastes like bread and wine but that are bread and wine no longer, having been changed by the words of the priest into Christ himself. He remains with us, present in the Blessed Sacrament, hiding "in leaf-light housel his too-huge Godhead."[7]

It is in a church that we bring our lives to him in sorrow, in love, with thanksgiving and supplication in the supreme offering of the Mass. A domestic church is a home where the ordinary business of living also goes on (though Mass is not usually celebrated there), where meals are cooked and eaten, where there is talking, laughing, reading, watching TV, playing games, cleaning up, or where woodwork is painted and the garden dug, in an underlying awareness of the generosity of God. A domestic church is a home where everything is ultimately seen in a wider context, despite the occasions of anger and argument, selfishness, and, from time to time, incomprehension. That phrase emphasizes the relationship between God and his creation, through which God—rather like a lover, to use a human analogy—wants to know everything about his beloved. It also refers, however, to the domestic, the everyday. Our religious life is not to be kept in a wardrobe like our best clothes, only to be brought out on special occasions! It needs to permeate all we do. The Church tells us that this is what God wants. Of course, he knows us individually better than we know ourselves, but we still want to tell him about ourselves; we believe that he wants to hear our hopes, our difficulties, and our fears, in the way that we tell (for the most part) those we love.

The communion between husband and wife is not a simple matter. There must be a realization of the value of each of them—including that of the woman in her role as wife and mother, and I say that because her qualities are sometimes seen only in her efforts in the world of work, outside the home. It is proper that women have "adequate access to public functions, which have generally been reserved for men"—including education.[8] But the high importance of women as wives and mothers should not be downplayed in order to emphasize their roles in paid employment. John Paul II affirms that, while women have the same right as men "to perform various public functions, society must be structured in such a way that wives and mothers are not in practice compelled to work outside the home."[9] In fact, thanks to better nutrition, clean water, and medical science, women, in affluent countries anyway, are living longer with energy and vigor. When their children no longer need them on a day-to-day basis, mothers of even large families have many years in which to pursue their interests. Secular agencies should ensure that a woman's years of child caring are taken into account as valuable experience to add to her qualifications.

Children, even adolescents, love to have their mother at home (though they do not always admit it, even to themselves). She brings a particular quality by being there as the ground on which the family is built, not having to strive anxiously to give the children the odd hour of "quality time" that no one really believes in. Husbands may have to consciously learn to appreciate the role of their wives in nurturing the family in the home, which in the long run may well provide more help and security than a decent salary. If wives and mothers were paid separately for all the jobs they do, they would earn a handsome salary. Should wives and mothers wish or find they need to take outside employment or pursue a profession while their children are young, it is certainly up to the husbands to make sure that their wives do not have to work an eighty-hour week, outside and inside the house. In Genesis, Eve is described as a "helper" for Adam. But before we see this as a put-down for women, let us remember that in the Old Testament, God is repeatedly called "my help," or "my helper," notably in the Psalms. Adam—that is, man—has in turn to be a helper to his wife.

The value of the man as husband and father must never be discounted. He is necessary to his wife and children as well. He is not just needed as provider but as true friend and loving intimate and confidant of his wife and teacher of his children, guiding them by his example and giving them his time, as well.

The creation of the domestic church is an individual affair. Where both husband and wife share religious faith, it is obviously a more open commitment. In any case, it is an intention, an aspiration, and a handing over to God of all that goes on in the family, which can be concretely established by a morning offering of the day, in such words as:

> Dear Lord, we (I) offer you this day all our (my) thoughts, words, actions, and sufferings because of the love of your Sacred Heart for us. We (I) offer everything for the souls in purgatory, that they may soon be in your presence, for the sake of our family, for the Holy Father and the Church, and for the world.

The old custom of grace before and after meals is an excellent way of bringing to mind our dependence on God and his words; according to the psalmist, "My people shall be filled with my good things." A classic grace, not long enough to cause the food on the table to get cold, goes:

> Bless us, O Lord, and these your gifts, which we about to receive through your bounty, through Christ our Lord. Amen.

Afterward, we can say:

We thank you, Lord, for these your gifts, which we have received through your bounty, through Christ our Lord. Amen.

"Bounty"—rich and free giving! Then add the briefest prayer for the souls in purgatory:

May the souls of the faithful departed, through the mercy of God, rest in peace. Amen.

I am convinced that that momentary pause for prayer is rich spiritually and culturally. It means, incidentally, that no one starts grabbing the food before the proper time and a few seconds of calm ensue before the meal begins.

If both spouses can pray together, the evening is a good time for prayer. A brief look at the day, individually, perhaps silently; an act of sorrow for sin; gratitude expressed for God's blessings—family not least; a prayer for individuals and for their own needs; and the guardian angels and patron (and favorite) saints invoked. The last words spoken in the Night Prayer of the Church are: "The Lord grant us a quiet night and a perfect end"—a good note to sleep on.[10]

Baptism

In the last chapter, we spoke of the arrival of the first child, the excitement, the responsibility for a little one, and the love he or she engenders. The next big day for the family is his or her Baptism.

When we bring our children to be baptized, we are performing a breathtakingly significance act. This innocent baby is human from the first and therefore shares in "fallen human nature," the result of that original sin described in Genesis and all too easily observed in ourselves and others. Baptism brings all who receive it "into the realm of the freedom of the children of God, to which all men are called." As we grow older, temptations to choose self come in thick and fast, and yet, as we are baptized, we can call on the grace of God to help us to choose the good instead of anything else, no matter how seductive. God is giving the "grace of salvation" even to a baby who cannot accept the gift for himself. He is baptized in the faith of his parent(s). The *Catechism* says that "the Church and parents would deny a child the priceless grace of becoming a child of God were they not to confer Baptism shortly after birth."[11] Baptizing babies goes back to the early Church—there is evidence from the second century of infant Baptism, and in the Acts of the Apostles the "whole households" who were baptized must surely have included babies.

It was once the custom to baptize babies on the day after their birth, or at least within the next few days. Thank God there are now far fewer risks to the survival of the baby, with the advances in hygiene and medicine. I would guess that nowadays it would only be because of an unusual medical emergency that a mother could not attend her baby's Baptism. But because the urgency is diminished, some parents come to feel that Baptism is something that can wait until the time when everything is running smoothly in the home and the mother feels up to arranging the party afterward.

Baptism is a real occasion for celebration, not just an opportunity to dress up the baby. Baptism is the new birth after birth and the beginning of the child's spiritual life—though, of course, the baby does not at the time understand it. When the Holy Father baptized babies on the Feast of the Baptism of the Lord in 1989, he described Baptism as a "fundamental and transforming event" in which the "merits of the Redemption effected by Christ...are applied to man.... [It] confers sanctifying grace, which eliminates original sin, and restores participation in God's actual trinitarian life." The baptized infant, all unknowing, is in some way taken into the loving life of the three Persons in one God! Because the little one cannot yet comprehend it, she is baptized as we saw, in the faith of her parent(s). Just as they look after her physical needs and her need for cuddling and kisses, so they look after her spiritual needs by presenting her to the Lord, as our Lady and St. Joseph presented Jesus in the Temple, offering the child to God and thus identifying him with the Jewish people. Christ has given us Baptism as a sacrament, a means of grace as we saw in chapter two, an entry into the life of the Catholic Church. After baptizing the babies, Pope John Paul II said:

> Dear parents and godparents, you have and will have the primary responsibility for the Christian education of these babies. You must give them a gradual understanding of the supernatural values of the Baptism which they now receive. Be faithful to this mission and responsibility! Pray for them each day to our Lady, their guardian angel, and their patron saint, so that faith and grace, symbolized by the lighted candle and the white robe, may accompany them throughout their lives and they may thus be serene and consistent witnesses to God's love and to salvation in Christ.[12]

To take on the role of godparent is a serious matter.

Strictly speaking, the Church requires only one godparent—a Catholic who has been confirmed and practices the faith. In practice, two are customary. There may be no more than two godparents, one male and one female. Baptized non-Catholics (other than those from the Orthodox Churches, who may be godparents) may serve as "Christian witnesses" to Baptism along with a Catholic godparent—though clearly it would be unsuitable to ask someone who was not sympathetic to the Catholic Church! The choice of godparents is important because they will be there to reinforce the parents' religious education of their child. That is in the future. For the moment, dressed in a special christening robe, the baby will be held by his or her mother. The *Catechism* explains that as Baptism liberates a human being from evil and from its "instigator, the devil," so first an exorcism is spoken over the little one, and oil is put on his or her head (athletes competing in the Olympic games used to rub oil on their bodies to strengthen them) to signify that he or she is getting ready for Baptism. Next, the blessed water is poured three times over the baby's head, in the name of the Father, the Son, and the Holy Spirit. Afterward, the baby is anointed again, this time with the perfumed chrism that was blessed on Holy Thursday in the diocesan cathedral, and this points to a later anointing at the sacrament of Confirmation, which actually completes the sacrament of Baptism. The baby, like any adult being baptized, wears a white garment as a sign that he or she has risen with Christ and has a share in his victory over sin and death. A candle is lit from the big Easter candle to show that this newly baptized baby has become, with other Christians, a light to enlighten everyone he or she meets—when that baby is old enough! His or her own baptismal candle takes its special place in the house, which is the domestic church.

What About Those Who Are Not Baptized?

The *Catechism* points out that "God...is not bound by his sacraments," so that people who have not heard of Christ or who have not received real teaching about him, but seek the truth and do "the will of God, in accordance with [their] understanding of it, can be saved."[13] Children who have died without Baptism are entrusted by the Church "to the mercy of God," remembering the words of Jesus, "Let the children come to me, do not hinder them."[14] In an emergency, anyone can baptize, whether Catholic or not. Even someone not himself or herself baptized can baptize in an emergency, as long as he or she intends to do that which the Church does. If one pours water on the person to be baptized or immerses that person in water and says, "I baptize you in the name of the Father, and of the Son, and of the Holy Spirit," that person, baby or adult, has received the sacrament. The need for Baptism will be in the mind of a Catholic parent. The Church takes this so seriously that there is all the more reason for parents to bring their child for Baptism as soon as they can.

Passing on the Faith

Parents are the first educators of their children. Part of their care for the child includes the desire to pass on to the child the truths of the Catholic faith. This responsibility cannot be wholly entrusted even to a Catholic school when the time for schooling arrives. Catholic education is not only learning *about* the faith; it is living the faith, and if parents do not play their part, no school or religious education class is likely to be able to do it for them. The parents' part consists primarily in doing their best to live Christian lives, striving to live the life of Christ in the world. They have to find the way to achieve this, by coming to understand the moral demands made on everyone, first of all by God and second by his Church, by examination of conscience and regular and honest sacramental confession.[15] To use an absurd example, it is no good committing a robbery on a Friday and going to Mass and receiving Holy Communion on Sunday without true repentance and the reception of the forgiveness of God in Confession on the intervening Saturday (which would be a very sudden conversion and would leave no time for restitution)! The smaller faults, which are everyday matters for most of us, also require recognition, repentance, and a real intention to try to conquer them. The sacrament of Reconciliation is our best help in the face of our human weakness, and the frequent reception of this means of grace is an ongoing requirement, especially during Advent and Lent as a good preparation for Christmas and Easter. This continuing life of sacramental prayer will lead at a later stage to ensuring that the child receives proper education in the faith, either in a Catholic school or in religious education classes and, most importantly, in the home. A little but useful book called *Helping Your Child to Pray* is a good preparation for formal instruction.[16] Preparation for the sacraments of Reconciliation and Holy Communion are, again, a matter for formal teaching and also require the support of the parents' commitment to the sacraments. Catholic parents need to show that both these sacraments matter to them, that they go regularly to Mass and to Confession, that they believe in them as realities of grace, and that they have recourse to them regularly in the pattern of their lives. Alongside this, a dialogue between parents and son or daughter in the context of love and faith teaches both formally and by example. Where only one parent is Catholic, that parent has to do the best he or she can "within the unity of [the] partnership"—the phrase used in all applications for the celebration of a mixed marriage—to pass on the Catholic faith to his or her children, while never denigrating the other parent's position. In addition, to quote a document of Vatican II, children should be taught that "man is more precious for what he is than for what he has."

As children grow, they can be shown that every subject becomes part of Christian formation: the intricacies of scientific exploration, nature's beauty, and the glory of the cosmos; human beings and their relationships and ways of living, in past times and in the present; literature and drama, the plastic arts, and the harmonies and dissonances of music. This is not done by a narrow and rigid slide rule, but by understanding God's loving creation and man's potentialities in it, which one uses for good or ill.

At the right time, that is, after the latency period, parents should lead their children to a true understanding of their sexuality and God's plan for it. It is very important that parents make sure that what their children are being taught in school follows Catholic teaching. They retain the right to withdraw their children from classes that they judge are inappropriate. An excellent book for adults, *Good News about Sex and Marriage* by Christopher West, a married layman, sets out and explains the Catholic understanding of sexuality in a very clear way.[17] *Theology of the Body Made Simple* by Fr. Anthony Percy is another wonderful resource for adults interested in learning more about John Paul II's teaching about human sexuality,[18] and *God's Plan for You* by David Hajduk is an excellent introduction to the teaching for young adults.[19] Those interested in pursuing the Theology of the Body at a more serious level will enjoy John Paul II's own text, *Man and Woman He Created Them: A Theology of the Body,* as well as Christopher West's comprehensive study titled *Theology of the Body Explained.*[20] A book called *Beyond the Birds and the Bees* is also a very useful resource for parents, with pages for children themselves when parents decide the time is right.[21]

Living in the Domestic Church

If their faith is in the forefront of their concerns, parents will not forget it in the middle of everyday activities with their child. A picture of our Lady and the Child Jesus, a statue of the Christ Child, St. Joseph, or a patron or favorite saint can become something special for even the youngest toddler. Stories of Christmas and a proper Advent calendar (not one full of chocolates) can appeal to a small child. Parents want their son or daughter to know that God loves him or her even more than his mommy and daddy do, and this can be indicated by stretched-out arms: "I love you higher than the sky! And God loves you higher than anything." Hugs will follow as the night the day!

In his book *Children Behaving Badly: Could My Child Have a Disorder?* Alan Train suggests to parents that even if they do not have a religious faith, they should bear in mind that religion may be able to help a child who is disturbed or has a disorder relating to hyperactivity, antisocial behavior, or difficulties in communication, among others. He says that because the child may often be unable to cope with him or herself and with others, he or she needs someone "who will always be there for him." Saying prayers each day, Train suggests, can assist the child in focusing on something outside him- or herself.[22] This seems to me just as true for children without specific difficulties and with Christian parents. Being human is a complicated matter; even a small child can feel layers of conflicting desires and emotions. He (or she) loves his mother so much that when she comes back after having left him perfectly happy for half a day, he may be cross with her because he remembers that she had the nerve to leave him! Gently introduced to the idea of a loving God, who is always there and whose love is unchanging, he can feel comforted and calmed. That special time when the child is ready for bed is the moment to "lift up the mind and heart to God." "Dear God, thank you for today. God bless Mommy, Daddy, me," is the place to start. The little one can soon learn that Jesus' mother, who is also our mother (even mom and dad's mom), loves us too and will pray for us—a gentle presence, unharassed and unharassing.

The child's guardian angel, his or her own special angel, is also someone he or she will feel safe with. Angels are spirits, messengers of God (hence pictured with wings for getting about quickly) whom God sends to look after each person, no matter how little, and to guide him or her in all ways. A prayer to the child's guardian angel can be: "Angel of God, my guardian dear, to whom God's love commits me here, ever this day [night] be at my side, to light and guard, to rule and guide. Amen."

In my parish, I am privileged to help with the children's liturgy on Sunday morning, where after a simplified reading of the Gospel and questions and explanations, the children draw individual pictures. These pictures are then stuck onto one big picture, which is taken up to the altar as the children's offering to God when we return to the church at the offertory of the Mass. One Sunday, a little boy, described by his mother as being "in a mood," did not want to join in or do anything. The others sat down to draw angels, so I said to little Jack, "Come and draw an angel. Drawing angels is a well-known remedy for moods; it makes you feel better." So he did draw an angel, his bad mood vanished, and he was perfectly cheerful for the rest of the Mass!

Perseverance in going to Mass every Sunday and on Holy Days of Obligation, however difficult at first, is really essential to the establishment of a spiritual life for the parent(s) and for the child. Most Catholic churches nowadays have a family Mass, which may be noisy but is at least welcoming. It is sad if, as sometimes happens, older members of the congregation resent the chatter and disruption of children—after all, we know our Lord did more than put up with them; he welcomed them and said, "Do not forbid them," and I don't suppose that the children of Galilee were less noisy or better behaved than ours. The Mass is the Mass. It is not a soothing ritual for the intolerant. Tactful parents will do their best to teach their children that church is a place for being quiet (though the children may notice that adults are speaking and singing at the tops of their voices!) and will take a child who is really screaming to a cry room, especially if the noise occurs during the consecration or the homily, but only for the length of time necessary for reasonable calm to be restored.

Some years ago in my parish, our parish priest was a retired bishop. One day he heard a cross old lady berating a young mother because her child was noisy during Mass. The poor mother was almost in tears. The next week in his newsletter, the bishop wrote, "When I hear a baby crying in church, it is music to my ears, because it means that the mother knows how important it is to come to Mass even with a fractious baby." In the parish, a baby's crying is known to this day as "the Bishop's music."

It is obviously good for parents to go to Mass together, even if one of them is not a Catholic. To share the experience of prayer has been shown time and again to cement the love of husband and wife for each other and their children. Even where one of the parents has no religious faith, the fact of their being together where they are able to remove themselves from the immediate cares of living can be a refreshment.

Marking the Seasons in the Domestic Church

The whole of the Church's year is marked by feasts and the fasts that prepare us for feasts. The Church's year starts in

November with Advent, the time of preparation for Christmas. The Church at this time looks back to the expectant longing of the Jewish people in the Old Testament. Like them, we wait with hope for the coming of the Messiah, amid the rush of gift buying and wrapping. There is no obligatory fasting nowadays in the Church calendar, except for Ash Wednesday and Good Friday, but one way to prepare for the coming of Christ at Christmas is to deny ourselves some goody—a small symbol of our sorrow for our shortcomings, which will in fact do us some good!

During Advent, St. Nicholas, the original Santa Claus, has his feast on December 6. In some parts of Christendom, splendid Santa Clauses are constructed—each one with an apple or an orange body, a walnut with a face drawn on it and a cotton wool beard attached, and a gold paper miter on his head (he was the Bishop of Myra)—and they make a splendid show. St. Lucy's feast is on December 13, in the darkest time of the year, and children can make glittering tinsel crowns and carry candles (with parents close at hand) to lighten the house in her honor.

Advent is different from Christmas, though our society tends not to think so. In the preparation during the former time (including going to Confession, which will help smooth away with forgiveness those faults of irritation inherent in the rush), we can relish the expectant darkness, and when the Christmas tree at last goes up, properly on Christmas Eve, we are ready for the angels, the star, and the Christ Child laid in the manger in our domestic crib. The crib is essential, large or small, simple or elaborate. The Three Wise Men (if available) can start their journey at the other side of the room, arriving at the crib on the feast of Epiphany.[23] At Christmas, our celebration is first a religious one, universal among Christians everywhere, and then a family one, because Christ himself came on earth to live in a family.

Lent, of course, is the penitential season of the year, where some form of self-denial is asked of us. This is a very appropriate time to approach the sacrament of Reconciliation.[24] There is, however, no point in it if the self-denial is merely intended to get our weight down or "detox," in the current jargon. There is a sophisticated view that says, "How can giving up cigarettes or sweets be relevant to the tremendous sacrifice of Calvary—even if one gives the savings to a charity?" Well, there is nothing to stop us from doing much more! Every Friday of the year is a remembrance of Good Friday. When the Church lifted the ban on eating meat on Friday (because in the wider Church outside the more affluent West, few people ever had meat to eat on a regular basis, anyway), she recommended some small sacrifice to be made each Friday and, as in Lent, real attention to prayer.

I am not sure whether it has been definitively decided whether Easter eggs are supposed to represent the new life of nature in spring or the stone the angels rolled away from the tomb—perhaps both elements have a place. In any case, we share in the new life of Easter, the redeemed life Christ won for us. An Easter egg hunt in the garden after lunch is somehow the perfect follow-up to the fresh glory of the Easter Mass.

Faith, excitement, rejoicing—all these go together. Flowers before a picture of our Lady in her month of May keep her in our minds. Children love it if there are some flowers in the garden that they are allowed to pick for our Lady. If there is no garden, perhaps they can arrange a bunch of bought flowers. Where a parish has processions around the block or around a garden in honor of the Mother of God and for the Blessed Sacrament feast of Corpus Christi, these bring a sense of awe and beauty to everyone who participates, and children especially love to strew petals before the Blessed Sacrament or the statue of Mary. Such events tap into a very deep vein of faith, though it is important that children are taught the sacredness of the event.

Cheerfulness is an essential ingredient of the domestic church. Inevitably, members of the family are not going to have fixed grins on their faces at all times. But with love of many kinds between them, cheerfulness will often break through. On that basis of love, each can give and also take, and all members can feel confident in the God-given, encircling but not stifling, experience of the family.

For Further Exploration

1. In the media, ordinary families are often denigrated as dull or hypocritical unless they are filled with wacky people. However, ordinary families really aren't all that dull! The family is a fascinating edifice, continually being added to and refurbished. Christian families, who see their lives in the context of God's gift of life and creation, always have further horizons to explore. In what ways do you think they can do this?

2. How does participating in Mass on Sundays and Holy Days of Obligation help individuals and couples to grow and mature as human beings?

3. What about prayer in the home? In what ways can we use it to remind ourselves of our immortal destiny?

4. The Baptism of a baby results in his or her everlasting relationship with the three Persons of the Trinity. What are some ways that parents can strive to make their children aware of this relationship, even at a young age?

5. Do you think there is value in celebrating feasts and fasts of the year? Why or why not? How might celebrating feasts and fasts enrich a family's relationship with God—both in the present and the future?

REFLECTION

Consider your own commitment to prayer. For most of us, prayer is not easy, but we can be reassured by the saying of the late Cardinal Basil Hume that if you mean to pray, you're praying! Brainstorm some realistic and creative ways you could make prayer a part of your everyday life.

CHAPTER 8

Difficulties

It is said that the wife of a former Archbishop of Canterbury was asked whether in the course of her many years of marriage she had ever thought of divorce. She replied, "Divorce, never. Murder, often." Getting along together is not always easy!

It is also misleading to suggest that a couple can solve all problems by themselves. Couples who admit God into their marriage and continually speak to him of their happiness and their sorrow, their cheerfulness and their bewilderment, can be certain of his grace to grace their mutual love.

The way in which a man and woman prepare for marriage is very important. If they place their growing love before God as a gift to him; if they prepare seriously for their marriage, thinking about what it means and the importance of family life and the upbringing of children; and if they follow the teaching handed on by the Church and wait for marriage before sexual intimacy, it gives them tremendous strength and makes infidelity, for instance, much less likely. Their life of faith, especially if it is shared, ensures continual reference to God and indeed to our Lady, the greatest woman who ever lived, who is always ready to pray for us in our perplexities.

Magazines and newspapers often report on couples, whether married or not, in which one or both of the members find themselves bored with the relationship. One of them is often quoted as saying, "The relationship wasn't going anywhere."

Of course, it is true that relationships can become stale and dull—same people, same employments and leisure activities. But as to "not going anywhere," that is a flawed analysis. Everything that is alive, and especially everything that concerns human beings, is always going somewhere. Growth, maturity, and death (from which a greater life comes—the grain of wheat dies unless it is planted in God's good soil)—are part and parcel of everything that has life. From a Christian standpoint, however, dullness is just a temporary emotion that can make us feel low but has little truth about it. A married life, just like an unmarried life, is always on the way to the City of God. The life of the Christian is literally a pilgrimage, a hard and tiring journey that begins with our first faltering steps and continues until we lie down in death. Each day we can see whether we have moved forward or back. Hard, yes; tiring, yes; but not dull. Through prayer and, where possible, the reception of the sacraments, life's journey is a continual exploration. Much depends on it, and for the vast majority of people this pilgrimage includes times of great happiness and contentment. Married people have a companion for the journey: someone who can affirm them as no one else can once they cease to be children. A "companion" literally means someone we eat with. With married couples, shared meals are an integral part of life—and for Catholics such meals remind us of the eucharistic food. Even if one of the two does not have a religious faith, the two are in it together.

Married couples need to take active steps not to take each other for granted. "Please" and "thank you," kisses of welcome and farewell, are important markers of the relationship. They serve, rather as prayers do, to remind us of love in our day-to-day life. Longer periods of time just spent together are a refreshment and a help, though it is not always easy to arrange them in the hurly-burly of work and family life. Even a comfortable half an hour in each other's company, without telephone calls or even children, can serve to restore husband and wife to each other.

Both need to take pains to look good when they go out together and not to be too slovenly or slatternly even in the house, though I am not suggesting diamonds at breakfast time. Most people, I believe, feel better when they are relatively clean and tidy.

However, even if they follow this to the letter, it does not mean that difficulties, irritations, separate and sometimes opposed concerns will not occur and present them with conundrums that cause anger and feelings of aloneness. Events outside their relationship with each other may strike: bereavement, accident, or illness—a trauma that batters them in such a way that their sorrow, bewilderment, or hurt seems to force them apart. The sheer exhaustion of the parents caring for a disabled child or a couple looking after an elderly parent almost inevitably increases tensions between the spouses. These can sometimes reveal the weaknesses of husband and wife, which add to the strain and distress. Work is another source of anxiety, both about performance in the job and the people we work with. Do they like us? How do they rate us? These are troubles that also impinge on our life at home.

On the other hand, the absence of work that we need can also be a strain. Unemployment is often a cause of depression, because it seems to impute both inadequacy and guilt, even if the matter was simply decided by other people (the bosses) and is no reflection on the individual. Someone may have been well thought of at work and yet lose a job. The feeling of rejection is sometimes hard to bear, and this inevitably affects a spouse. At home, as we saw in an earlier chapter, a mother with a new baby can also feel worried as well as tired.

Is there a certain way of banishing this sort of difficulty? The first step is to place our stresses and strains before the loving Sacred Heart of Jesus, both the symbol and the reality of divine love. Having done that humbly and with sorrow for the faults that have been committed, it is necessary for spouses to be as open as possible with each other. The husband may be impatient, possibly judging that he sees a clear path to a solution, and if he is not listening properly to his wife, he may be baffled as to why she is not doing what he sees so clearly to be right. (He may objectively be wrong, of course.) She, on the other hand, may feel overwhelmed by her awareness of peripheral issues and either hesitate long before making a decision or make it in a devil-may-care frame of mind, which she may well regret. The old business of trying to see and understand the other's point of view is really essential.

Happy Families Past

Family anecdotes reveal the content of many families in earlier times. A speaker at a neighborhood society meeting told of being introduced to a very old lady who had lived as a child in a small cottage with an outside lavatory, the very house, now much developed and very valuable, in which the speaker himself lived. There were fourteen of them in the old lady's family, and she recalled her life there as "very happy"! The rich and the very poor probably led lives that were much more disordered than those of the bourgeoisie, craftsmen and tradesmen. The old lady's father had been a tradesman. Other stories from earlier generations reveal that there was often a great deal of homemade fun—games, music, plays acted in the parlor. A friend who was a child in the 1920s recalled her large family clustered around the harmonium, on which one brother would play hymns while they all joined in with great vigor. The downside to the availability of so much slick and glossy professional entertainment, day and night, is that there is little reason for the family to amuse itself through activities, parents and children together, thus strengthening the bonds between them all. Large families became little worlds of their own. It is often noted that unhappy parents make for unhappy children, so evidence that the children were happy (most of the time) is of great importance.

Faithfulness

Until the middle years of the twentieth century, marriage was an almost universally admired institution in the United States; divorce was relatively uncommon and quite difficult to get, and infidelity carried its own risks. Now, people without a Christian (or, indeed, Jewish) understanding of marriage as a graced lifelong commitment often take infidelity lightly, apparently without any understanding of its effects.

Sometimes trouble arises from the different ideas about the commitment of each to the other. It is possible that this is a particularly contemporary phenomenon because contemporary society in general no longer upholds the level of commitment to marriage that was largely accepted a hundred years ago. There were certainly men at that time who were unfaithful, some of whom would abandon their wives and families. Maltreated or abandoned wives were greatly pitied. Some unfaithful men would nevertheless wish to preserve the marriage (and even perhaps remain faithful thereafter). That must also have been difficult for any wife who knew about or suspected her husband's infidelity. On the other hand, there were without doubt also happy marriages, and marriage was accepted as an honorable estate. Attitudes to marriage have now changed. Divorce laws in the last forty years have made marriage breakdown seem ordinary and perfectly acceptable, and changing a spouse hardly more difficult than changing a house.

The best way to deal with the temptation to infidelity is not to give in to the first stirrings of it, but to run away from it. To face it in a heroic manner often leads to defeat and to giving in. To avoid situations where one will be drawn to the person who has taken one's eye is the most courageous course. As we saw earlier, infidelity brings great unhappiness. The one who remains faithful loses feelings of self-esteem and is deeply hurt, and this in turn can affect the children, even if they have, quite rightly, not been told about the matter. The one who betrays damages him-

or herself, one's spouse, any children, and the wider family. No pleasure justifies it, and it is a very serious sin. Unfaithfulness also begins in the will.

By the grace of God, a repentant offender can be forgiven through the sacrament of Reconciliation. Someone who does not share in the faith can nevertheless ask God for forgiveness and receive grace to help him or her not to offend again. To make a sacramental confession, with sorrow for one's sins and a firm intention not to sin again (particularly in the ways that are the greatest temptation to us), brings a certainty of forgiveness. The discipline of regular reception of this sacrament of Reconciliation with God continually brings us up short against our temptations, of whatever kind.

Money Worries: Who Pays for What?

Worries about money can also lead to trouble in marriage. Another area of difficulty that often leads to wrangling lies in the allocation of money, not just the misuse of it but the "who pays for what?" Which of the two is to have primary responsibility for providing for the family? If both husband and wife work, as is certainly the case where there are no children and may well be the case after the children are born, how are they to share the money? Are they simply going to pool it, each keeping a certain amount for day-to-day spending, or are they going to divide it along the lines of "I'll pay the mortgage and you can pay the housekeeping"? Can they agree on how much each can keep for personal expenses, pleasures, and presents? What happens if one of them loses his or her job? Should they have contingency plans for this sort of event? If one of them has an expensive hobby or has been deeply committed to supporting a particular charity, how are these facts to be accommodated?

Then there are the heartrending stories where a husband or wife has run up tremendous debts, without the other knowing and with devastating consequences for the family. There are many different ways in which this can happen. Gambling, of course, is one of them; another is the overuse, or too easy use, of credit or store cards; and another is spending too much money on a hobby. Where it affects the relationship between the couple, honesty is the only possible course. In such cases, it is sensible to call in specialist help, perhaps through debt counselors.[1] Each of the two has a duty to try to discern the worries of the other, to support the other in any way possible, and also to tell the truth about his or her own behavior; this is unlikely to be achieved without pain. The value of the marriage is something that husbands and wives need to keep in mind, no matter what the difficulties.

The Marriage Journey

When someone falls in love, the beloved seems to be lovable, worthy of love and thus beautiful, interesting—even exciting— kind, and generous. Both of them seek to get to know the other well and are wise not to rush into marriage. Both need to be convinced that their initial perception of the other remains and survives the learning process. If it does not do so, the relationship can fade away. It may seem strange, but this time of discernment will yield much better understanding if it is not led as a "pseudo-marriage," because besides the happiness of knowing that this is the way of the Catholic world, in friendship with God, the bonding effect of sexual intimacy serves to cloud the ability to see what the other is really like. It disrupts the learning process and falsifies perceptions. The wisdom of the Church's teaching is visible here as well.

St. Augustine in the fifth century describes in a very pertinent way the three "goods" of marriage ("goods" here means something like treasures or blessings of marriage): children, the faithful loyalty of the two, and the bond between them, which is like the bond between Christ and the Church and cannot be broken.

These "goods" are things to be kept in mind on the journey to assist in the avoidance of pitfalls.

The two people prepare with seriousness in order to marry before God, their families, and friends, and embark happily on the journey. But almost at once they may come across difficulties in their new state of life. They have to discover a *modus vivendi*. Many marriage preparation courses include lists of questions that the individuals answer separately, and this can provide some guidance on the way they would like their married life to be. If both are working, how much should each do in the house? What about evenings out separately—are they acceptable to each, or not? The man and woman can be deeply in love and yet have very different interests, and these can provide interesting crosscurrents in their relationship—as long as they do not take over all the energies of the individual. There are lots of good ways of living for a married couple, but at the start of their married life it may be helpful to clarify certain expectations of each.

In the course of this journey, each begins to glimpse those characteristics of the other that he or she wishes to keep hidden, or may indeed be unaware of. Everyone has these—it is part of the fallen human condition. Some of them may be inherited, some the result of the individual's own upbringing. How secure was each person as a baby in attaching to his or her mother? How did one feel as a child about one's father or siblings? If the nurturing was inconsistent, it may well have had the effect of producing a continuing anxiety, especially about attachments in general, and thus, perhaps particularly, about one's spouse. This in turn may lead to suspicion and jealousy, or domination and attempts at limiting the other. One or the other may long for a version of the uncomplicated love of mother for baby—baby's simple needs for food, warmth, and cuddles! However, "infancy never comes again": neither husband nor wife is "parent" to the other.[2] The need for reassurance, at any time, may lie with either husband or wife. The longing for affirmation is one of the deepest seated wishes of the human heart, so spouses need to be delicate in their perception of the other's need. When a person is under stress, he or she is likely to regress to an earlier stage of development and require more support. It may happen that both want assurance of their worth at the same time—and each may have to deny self for the sake of the other. In a sense, their roles do resemble those of parents, though they are not parents, in that each can support the other in their steps to self-actualization. The job of parents is to help their children stand on their own feet, step by step, year by year. Spouses have to uphold each other without making the other a pampered child. They have to accept that they are equal adults made in the "image and likeness of God." They are two in one flesh, but they remain individuals—and adults.

Mary Kirk, in her book *The Marriage Work-Out,* reproduces a diagram by Dr. Deirdre Morrod that sets out six stages in a marriage from dependence, via independence, to interdependence. She sees marriage first in terms of romantic feelings, which give way in time to a sense of reality—when the irritating habits and negative feelings of the other come to loom large. This is followed, she suggests, by a power struggle between the two, which ends in each finding him- or herself. This leads to reconciliation, and in turn mutual respect and love win the day.[3] It is certainly true that husbands and wives will not always find themselves in agreement and, though perhaps "power struggle" carries the implication that one or other will be a victor, a power struggle does not necessarily end in both antagonists discovering themselves! Both of them certainly have to discern the times to give way and the times to insist. "All right, we will ask your father over for Christmas. But we really must have my old aunt; she has nowhere else to go!" "Yes, you should take that job in New York, but if I cannot find a decent job, the right schools, or if I really hate it, can we revisit the decision in two years' time?" Because the wife is in most cases the primary caregiver of the children, she is more likely to have to make adjustments in the matter of moves for work and so on. If the wife is the major earner, the negotiating will be more delicate still. Since the wife brings the children into the world, it is not unreasonable that the husband should see himself as provider and protector, however much the edges are blurred in the day-to-day world. Learning negotiating skills does give a sense of independence that will grow into interdependence as awareness of the other deepens and the two explore themselves and each other together.

Conflict in marriage is very common. It can be sparked by continuous irritations, but an effort of will can be enough in that case to dampen the annoyance, in view of the "goods" of the marriage as a whole. If both husband and wife can talk clearly, honestly, and as far as possible with love, problems between them are more likely to be resolved than if either one becomes angry and rancorous. Loving honesty about areas of conflict clearly communicated is probably more likely to resolve differences than rancorous exchanges and fights. It will not be easy to find resolutions, especially if the couple, for whatever reason, have gotten out of the habit of doing things together on a regular basis.

A very good suggestion made by Mary Kirk is that the spouse who is disturbed should describe his or her feelings without accusations. "When you come in late I feel...because...." This is much less likely to cause anger than the direct "Why do you...?"[4] This technique is viable even in serious matters: infidelity, jealousy, bullying, or concerns over money. It is also necessary to listen to the other's response and understand the feelings revealed in it. After that, some allowance or negotiation may be possible.

Can Psychology Help?

Psychologists come up with many and varied systems for coping with stress, and stress itself is a part of many and varied situations we encounter in life. Between spouses, whatever the conflict, feelings of hostility, disappointment, or bewilderment are likely to be strong. It may be that the first thing to do is to separate out thoughts from feelings. Feelings often color our thought processes. If our thoughts or judgments about an area of conflict are distinguished from our feelings about them, it may help us to view the matter in a calmer spirit. Psychologists call this process "isolation."

Another way is by logical analysis, which involves looking for explanations in a careful and systematic way, so that it is easier to formulate plans to improve the situation. This is also very relevant to married couples. If the argument is about money, an exploration of why the spendthrift spouse is behaving in this way is important. Is it because he or she is really short of something essential and therefore not thoughtless in paying out money? If so, an adjustment to the family finances may be possible. If, however, one of them is using money on frivolous things, like gambling, spending too much on drinking and dining, on buying fashion items, or even pursuing some particular interest, a calm analysis of where the money is going may bring the offender to a more reasonable view of the matter and a better understanding of what is reasonable in the circumstances. This is known as "rationalization."

As we have seen in many of these pages, empathy is very much in the forefront in the lives of married couples. Empathy is, strictly, the "ability to sense how others are feeling in emotionally-arousing situations so that our interactions take account of their feelings."[5] It may be that the one who is the life and soul of the party and flirts with everyone arouses strong feelings of jealousy or failure in the other—if he or she does not think about and perhaps modify this behavior. On the other hand, the one who sits in a corner and refuses to join in may embarrass or upset the other by appearing to be standoffish or disapproving. If one learns to feel with the other person in the marriage, allowances can be made; behavior can be modified if, for whatever reason, it genuinely causes pain to the other.

Playfulness is also suggested as a way to counter stress, and again, this is important in marriage. Most if not all marriages have a sort of internal library of words, jokes, songs, films, situations, and the like. Calling up one of these imaginary books is one of the real pleasures of long-lasting marriages, enabling couples to revisit the good things they have shared. It can also be useful in diffusing anger and strife, as long as it includes the other and is not dismissive of the concerns of the other. "That reminds me of...." "Do you remember the time...?" "Wasn't it funny when...?" Some situations may be too serious to submit to this treatment, but by no means all.

It is sometimes helpful to hold back thoughts or feelings until an appropriate time occurs to pursue them. Some couples may like to set up a particular time and place, possibly with a cup of coffee in hand (though nothing stronger, I would suggest), to mull over their concerns. This is a larger version of counting to ten before responding when anger is aroused.

Another quality can help couples to function in this imperfect and fallen world, and that is the ability to tolerate ambiguity, where it does not cut across the moral law. It can happen that a situation is so complex that it is impossible to make a clear choice. In those cases, it may be better to continue to function in a less than ideal way than to take action that would provoke a crisis possibly leading to fracture.

What Agencies Can Help?

Many couples in times of trouble long for someone to relieve them of the responsibility of resolving the conflict between them. Unfortunately, direct advice is unlikely to satisfy both parties! However, talking to someone outside the combat who is skilled in counseling techniques—that is, someone who is able to encourage both parties to be frank and speak openly and thereby come to see what the position of each really is, beyond anger or feelings of resentment—can be a genuine help. Retrouvaille is an international organization with a mission to support and help save marriages. Retrouvaille, which literally means "rediscovery," is a live-in weekend and post-weekend program for married couples. The emphasis is on a technique of communication between a husband and wife. Although it is a Catholic organization, it also welcomes couples of other faiths. The program offers a husband and wife the chance to rediscover themselves, their spouse, and a loving relationship within their marriage.

Many couples in difficulties rightly turn to a priest. Most priests are men of deep faith and integrity. They will have learned a great deal about the human condition from the experiences of their ministry. They can often bring us back to an awareness of God's love, to a new realization of the need for humility, and a recognition of the things that are sinful in our lives. Many problems in marriage are spiritual ones. Best of all, priests can absolve us from our sins. It is, however, no good expecting a priest to work miracles while the couple themselves make no effort to resolve their difficulties through prayer and the sacraments, as well as rational analysis and discussion.

Commitment

I heard an athlete being asked about his physical readiness for a particular race. "Well," he said, "athletics are all in the head!" By this, I think he meant that the level of commitment and determination was even more important than physical preparedness—though the latter was certainly necessary too. Similarly, marriages are all "in the head," in that the decision to marry is made both by the mind and by the will, and this decision is an ongoing one. Of course, it follows the mutual attraction that leads to love, and if someone is lovable, many difficulties can be overcome. "Lovable," of course, must apply to both parties. We often hear nowadays about very rich couples who make a "prenuptial agreement," by which they arrange the disposition of money, the who-gets-what, if they later decide to divorce! Surely if one feared that one's future spouse might steal one's belongings, one would do better to call the whole thing off at once! In Catholic terms, such an agreement would make the marriage null; it would not be a marriage, because it would imply that the decision to marry is a temporary one, that marriage is not for life, for better or worse until death. Real commitment and this quality of lovableness, which really means generosity toward the other, are at the root of marriage.

Commitment, as a root value in marriage, is for the Christian commitment to Christ. As a man and woman prepare for marriage, it will help them to make the gift of self to the other and to reinforce their openness to new life. When they have done that, the graces delivered by the sacrament will help them to be faithful. Again, if they are lovable, they are less likely to want anyone else and much less likely to give in to temptation. As we saw earlier, the society in which we live sees sexual pleasure as the be-all and end-all of love, while the Christian view is that love is an end in itself and sexual pleasure goes with it—not against it (as it does in the case of adultery). To repeat what was said earlier, adultery is always a betrayal of the self, a betrayal of the spouse, and not only the spouse but the children of the marriage as well.

Unfaithfulness by the husband is every bit as culpable as by the wife. Any old-fashioned notions that it was more or less all right for men were never accepted by Catholic teaching and were a flagrant injustice. Adultery is a misuse of human sexuality, which was given by God for his own good purposes and for the good of husband and wife. Communication is one important way that couples defend against unfaithfulness, as it leads to greater intimacy and understanding within the couple. Couples who manage their fertility by means of tracking the woman's cycle often reveal a much greater closeness to one another than other couples do, as working together in this way opens an extra channel of communication.

Violence, Hypocrisy, and Aggression

The findings of the July 2000 research report on domestic violence put out by the National Institute of Justice (U.S.) stated that nearly 25 percent of the women surveyed and nearly 7.5 percent of the men surveyed said they were raped and/or physically assaulted by a current or former spouse, cohabiting partner, or date at some time in their lifetime. More incidences of domestic violence are being reported each year, although many still go unreported. It may be because the cult of social freedom in our society leaves some people unable to deal with their emotions—accepted rules of behavior are less understood. The increase in violence is acknowledged even by the government, but the latter has not yet faced up to the difficulty of socializing young men who are often brought up without fathers and lack male role models. Despite the efforts of the feminist movement, some men see women simply as sexual objects, to be used merely for gratification and whose availability for sex is taken for granted. Through use of the contraceptive pill and acceptance of abortion, many women, longing for love, have accepted their role as compliant females and find themselves used and often subsequently rejected.

It used to be said that hypocrisy was the tribute that vice paid to virtue. Currently, hypocrisy is seen as one of the few unforgivable courses of action. Hypocrisy is indeed an ugly vice in a simple sense. To pretend to be generous when one is miserly, even faced with another's real distress, is clearly wrong. What happened, however, is that in avoiding hypocrisy, we see bad behavior blatantly paraded in the cause of honesty and frankness. Anything goes; one should do what one likes. As a result, the widely held, if not always observed, common code of conduct no longer exists. Violence in TV, films, and especially certain types of music may well condition young males— particularly in the absence of fathers—to believe that violence is an accepted course of action or response. This may in part be because they are usually the perpetrators in the media.[6]

Violence in the home, whether against women or against men, should not be left unreported to the police. It is a crime against the woman, or, more rarely, the man, and the perpetrator needs to realize the harm he or she has done. Violence can also be psychological, and in such cases the victim should seek help—initially, perhaps, from a priest or doctor.

Women, because of their entirely to-be-welcomed greater opportunities for participating in wider areas of life, are being led in some cases to see living in a debased male fashion as part of those greater opportunities. We certainly read of higher levels of violence and greater alcohol dependence among young women. Underneath this behavior, however, the same search for love can be discerned.

Our over-sexualized society and the easiness of divorce have produced a more fragmented culture, which includes cruelty to women, though women are said never to have been so prosperous and free. The fact of marriage itself sets a much higher standard for the spouses than looser forms of relationship and also gives them a greater investment in their way of life.

The great Russian writer Leo Tolstoy begins his novel *Anna Karenina* with the sentence: "All happy families resemble each other, but each unhappy family is unhappy in its own way." In this instance, he is wrong. Happy families are just as individual and just as interesting as unhappy ones.[7] As G. K. Chesterton pointed out, it is harder to be sane than to be mad, and the real excitement of the eight-thirty train from Clapham Junction to Waterloo is the fact that it arrives at Waterloo and not at Charing Cross! Every happy family travels to its destination and is not thrown off course. Every set of circumstances is different, even if only in detail, and the people themselves are unique individuals, even though they share many characteristics with others of their time, their sex, and their upbringing, including traits such as the depth of their religious faith, their unusual levels of anxiety, and many other factors. For Catholics, it is a comfort that the Church is a church of sinners, so that every good act is a little triumph against the odds.

Can one discern the qualities that make a marriage a happy one? A happy marriage can be described as one where, despite sadness, tension, and loss, there is continuing love and concern for the other, regardless of the human frailty, sins, and errors of both husband and wife. This love spills over into love of children, equal with the parents before God (the parents who are co-creators with him), yet in need of nurture and education, love and formation in the faith. The love a person has for his or her children is not the same as the love he or she has for husband or wife.

Love is different from liking. Indeed, there may well be times—though, please God, not too many—when individually we may not like our spouse or children ("Divorce, never; murder, often"), but we still love them because, deep down, we want their good, which is the true definition of love.

Faith As a Value in Marriage

A shared system of belief, a Christian understanding of the human situation, is of inestimable value. But belief itself is not enough. Each Christian couple will try to live their faith and to deepen it continually. Take it for granted, and in the jungle that is the world, belief itself may be choked and lost. Our love for God must underpin all our other loves. God alone gives us the freedom to love each other without drawing back. There is no solution without the grace given to us through prayer.

Sorrow and repentance are the marks of the greatest saints, the giants of Christian life. St. Peter, having betrayed the one he loved best, wept bitterly before them all.

Gaudium et Spes says that "man [inclusive] cannot fully find himself except through a sincere gift of himself."[8] This is the watchword for all married couples. Following it gives the best chance of a happy life together.

For Further Exploration

1. If a husband and wife gave free reign to their anger every time a difficulty arose, how would it affect their marriage? What techniques can husbands and wives use to help them face problems in their relationships?

2. How can jokes, having fun, and living again in memory things the couple have enjoyed together be helpful during difficult times?

3. In what sense can we say that "marriages are made in the head"?

4. From your own knowledge and observation, how would you describe a happy marriage?

REFLECTION

We are all flawed as human beings, and we continually need to struggle to break out of our selfishness toward others. How seriously do you take this? Do you try to do it on your own, without seeking God's help? If so, how does this affect your efforts? Your relationship with your spouse? Your relationship with God? The whole of creation points to God's love for each one of us. Name some ways to redirect your efforts to become less selfish, placing them in his hands.

CHAPTER 9

Married Saints and Their Witness

Saints are those souls who after death live in the glory of God in heaven. Where is heaven? Heaven is where God is, and yet God is everywhere! This sounds like a conundrum, but it arises because we think in terms of space and time, which encircle our world, marking its limits. But God is infinite and beyond these boundaries, which are part of his creation. God chose to come into our world when he sent his Son to limit himself within human dimensions, to live and die in time and space in the world, and to abolish all these limits by rising from the dead at the resurrection. The *Catechism* says that in Scripture "heaven" or the "heavens" refer both to the firmament and to God's "place."[1]

The saints, therefore, are those who after death and the cleansing of purgatory are with God. We have no idea how many of them there are, but our trust in God's mercy leads us to hope that there are millions upon millions of them. Some of these millions lived lives so clearly close to God that the Church, having studied all the evidence about them, feels she can state with authority that these people are in heaven. They are the people whom we call saints.

It is certainly true that a majority of the canonized saints and blesseds (who are on the way to sainthood) are priests or religious, both men and women. In a sense, they have a head start on the path, because they have given their lives directly to God and have turned all their energies toward his service. It is also a fact that canonization is an expensive process—not that the authorities in Rome are making big profits out of it, but the thoroughness of the investigation, the number of documents, and the cost of their preparation and dissemination is high. It is also easier to study the holiness and devotion of those who are priests or religious, because they have had spiritual directors and freely share their life of faith with other clergy or religious. (A "religious" is a monk, friar, brother, or nun.) They are known to others in their religious orders. It is, of course, much harder to discern the spiritual gifts of Mrs. Smith who lives down the street, but for all we know, after death she may be up there with St. Peter and St. Paul and St. Teresa of Avila and all the rest of the spiritual greats, even if she is not formally canonized by the Church.

However, there are many formally acknowledged saints who were married men and women in most centuries of the Church. The very greatest of all the saints was married and was a woman: her name is Mary, and she is the Mother of God. Her marriage was a real one, carried out according to the rites of the Jews of her day. Its uniqueness comes from the fact that her Son was divine and was conceived by the Holy Spirit. Her husband, Joseph, is a great saint as well.

When the angel Gabriel came to her and told her she would "conceive and bear a son," she responded immediately by asking how this was to be, "since I am a virgin." In a way, this was a strange response from a young girl who was betrothed. From this, the Fathers of the Church, the theologians and biblical scholars of the early centuries, deduced that Mary and Joseph had pledged themselves to marry and live together without the sexual expression of their love, giving up this great and joyous gift that leads to the birth of children, as a sacrifice to God.[2] Among the Jews, marriage was a duty, and there was no concept of the monastic life. After this pledge, the reality of Mary's conception must have been like a thunderbolt to Joseph. But his faith and humility were such that when the angel appeared to him, he was able to accept the reality of her virginal conception and to proceed with the marriage as they had intended. From the very earliest times, the Church has taught that Mary remained a virgin. Caught up in her relationship with God the Father and the unique conception of her Son, the Son of God made Man, she had given herself to God totally. Therefore, she lived her life with Joseph in her virginity, and he, for his part, as adoptive father of her Son, acquiesced with complete self-giving in the promise they had originally made to each other. Mary and Joseph must have loved one another greatly. Their life of prayer would have been overwhelming because of the intensity of their love for God, who had given them this unparalleled gift—his own Son to bring up. Yet Mary would have done all the wifely and motherly chores, happily and with enthusiasm and diligence. Joseph must have worked hard at his trade in order to look after Mary and his adopted Son, Jesus. He took them into exile to escape Herod's massacre and would have had to find employment in an alien place in order to support them and try to make them as secure as possible. Back in Nazareth, they would both have had the unique happiness of watching the Son of God grow from toddler to boy, "in grace and wisdom." They must have wondered then, in their happiness, why Simeon at the presentation in the Temple had foretold that a sword would pierce Mary's heart. Their joy was interrupted during these years only when they lost Jesus on the way back from Jerusalem and found him in the Temple, where they heard his disturbing words that he had to be about his Father's business. Thereafter, he came back to the carpenter's shop in Nazareth and "was obedient to them."[3] The two wonderful things about our Lady, as she is called in many languages, are her ready acceptance of God's will and her humility. Humility is often thought of as being either downtrodden or hypocritical. Yet to be humble means that one knows where one stands before God. The greater the love and the more intense the awareness of the divine, the greater is the humility.

"Here I am, the servant of the Lord," said Mary, "let it be with me according to your word."[4] She is so beautiful that many nations want to claim her as their own: Our Lady, *Notre Dame,* Madonna, *Unser Frau, Nuestra Señora,* and so on.

The wonderful thing about Joseph is his selfless generosity. He is not mentioned again in the Gospels, so it is assumed that he died some time during the quiet Nazareth years, most likely in the arms of Jesus. For this reason, he is known as the patron saint of those near death, the patron saint of a happy death. It is said that my grandmother on her deathbed greeted the doctor with disgust. "Oh," she said, "it's you. I thought you were St. Joseph come to fetch me." Such a gentle picture, so far removed from that of the grim reaper! St. Teresa of Avila maintained that to set up a new convent she needed two things: a house and a statue of St. Joseph, the guardian of the religious life and of the family.

The graceful image of the Holy Family is sometimes seen nowadays as some sort of slap in the face for ordinary couples. That is perverse! If God had meant everyone to emulate the way Mary and Joseph lived in the matter of sexuality, mankind would have come to a full stop! They were called to a special way of expressing their love, in the context of the amazing trust that God had placed in Mary, the virgin who had already dedicated herself to him. She had given God her heartfelt "yes" as the virgin she remained. Joseph's call to be guardian to the Son of God and his mother required a particular selflessness, which he must have prayed for and which he perfectly obtained. In Genesis, however, God tells everything he creates to "be fruitful and multiply," and he says it again when he creates human beings, male and female.[5] The life of Mary and Joseph can remind us that the married state holds the fullness of many different joys, expressed in different ways, and that sexual love, with the children that are its fruit, is God's will for the vast majority of people.

Our Lady provides the definitive break between the position of women in the ancient world and in Christianity. The Jewish mothers in the Old Testament had their own value, though it often seems not to have been spelled out.[6] The fact that some Jewish rituals took place in the home emphasized the importance of the Jewish mother. The ancient Greco-Roman world took little account of women. But pictures of Mary with her divine child softened the perceptions of what are sometimes called the Dark Ages, and she became revered by men and women alike.

Married Saints:
What Sort of People Are They?

The lives of the saints who were married men and women are as varied as the lives of people anywhere. They come from high social standing, even royalty, and from the very poor. Some were highly educated, some almost ignorant. Some had children, some were childless. In some cases, their marriages were not happy ones but were persevered in. In many other cases, they dearly loved their spouses and lived happily with them. What they have in common is their love of God, lived in whatever circumstances they had to face.

Their lives, however happy, in no way resemble the lives of those beloved of certain types of magazines that portray idealized portraits of the famous and materially fortunate. These are always described as being physically beautiful and as people who take care of their looks with an army of personal trainers, a home gym, and a level of devotion that would do credit to a Trappist monk. Their spouse, or "partner," has similar characteristics; the one or at most two children are perfect. Their houses are immaculate, their holidays exotic, their felicity complete. Apparently, they are secure from all worries, until some months later when we read that they have "split up," citing extreme cruelty, unreasonable behavior, incompatibility, or sheer nastiness. We begin to doubt the truth of the original picture. Real saints are not like such people in the papers,[7] since, though in very different ways, they all follow the two chief commandments: to love God and to love their neighbor, even as they love themselves.

The people described above are presented as those who look after themselves with great fervor. If the reports are accurate, the stars in question have almost certainly been barking up the wrong tree. Our saints are different from celebrity greats.

Brief Lives of Some Married Saints

St. Thomas More

In the sixteenth century, St. Thomas More, "the man for all seasons," was married twice. His first wife, Joanna or Jane, whom he married when she was sixteen, died, leaving him with four young children. Thomas More, already a busy and successful lawyer, looked almost at once for a second wife who would help in bringing up his children. He found her in Lady Alice Middleton, the widow of someone whom he had known. She was some eight years older than he, a forthright lady of no special beauty, but one who had a loving heart and a good, though perhaps not intellectual, mind. In later years, she looked after the land and farm for Thomas in his absences, helped by one of her sons-in-law. It is noticeable that when the More children married their spouses, they all tended to take up residence with Sir Thomas and Lady More in Chelsea.

Lady Alice brought her daughter from her first marriage to live with them and looked after them all, and, as St. Thomas wrote in his own epitaph, translated from Latin, she was "a rare distinction in a stepmother, was as affectionate as if the children were her own." He adds, "O how blessed if fate and religion had permitted all three of us to live together! I pray the tomb and heaven may unite us, thus death could give what life could not give."[8] Whether the ladies in question would have welcomed this arrangement on earth, had it been possible, is open to debate! It is a clear indication, however, that St. Thomas More was happy as a married man.

A foster child also lived with the family, and More educated all the children in the house with tutors he brought to the family home. One of these tutors later married Margaret, the foster child, while Meg, Thomas More's eldest daughter, a brilliant scholar, married William Roper, who had lodged with the family as a law student.

When the children were still young, the whole house became, as the Dutch humanist scholar Erasmus called it, "a Christian college." The girls and Thomas More's son, John, all learned together, although it was unusual for girls to be educated in England at that time. When he was away, Thomas More expected them to write to him in Latin; he replied, with genuine interest, in the same language.[9] The children were taught Greek as well as Latin; they studied literature, including poetry; the Scriptures, of course; philosophy; and history. In addition, they gained knowledge in subjects such as medicine, music, mathematics, and astronomy under, in some cases, distinguished tutors. Thomas also understood the importance of the enjoyment and engagement of children in their learning. They liked archery, so he put up the letters of the Greek and Latin alphabets as targets so that the children could learn them while they shot.[10]

Prayer and devotion were the basis of life in his house. Morning and evening prayers were said, and a reading from the Scriptures took place at dinner. After dinner, which was taken at midday, there was often music, as most of the family played one or two instruments and sang. Dame Alice was encouraged by Thomas More to practice her music, and although by all accounts she was her own woman and followed her own inclinations, she joined in and sang duets with Thomas. Homemade plays were also performed. Thomas More kept with him a fool, who was licensed to make fools of all around him, and Alice kept a monkey, who teased the dogs!

The house was also filled with visitors, scholars, dignitaries, lawyers, and students of law—and even the king himself on occasion. More was without illusions as to the king's friendship. When his son-in-law congratulated him on it, he said, "I have no cause to be proud. If my head could win him a castle in France, it should not fail to go." His marriage and his family life had a beauty of its own. Erasmus, who stayed with them, thought these years before the troubles were very happy and remarked that More lived sweetly and pleasantly with his wife, "as if she was as young and lovely as anyone could desire."

His care for his dependents reached to his servants and workers on the farm. McOustra quotes a letter from Thomas to his wife, written after a fire had destroyed farm buildings, in which he states that the farmers must not lose by it and that the workers should be kept on the payroll unless another job could be found for them.

Thomas More's own spiritual life supported him in the world and in the home. He spent long hours in prayer, and he attended Mass on weekdays whenever he could. When he was Lord Chancellor of England, the highest temporal post in the land after the monarch, he was rebuked with the following words by the Duke of Norfolk, who caught him serving Mass humbly in his parish church in Chelsea: "A parish clerk, my Lord Chancellor!"

Then came his time of suffering. The king sought an annulment of his marriage to Catharine of Aragon, both because he wanted a male heir, which she had not given him (her only surviving child was a girl, Mary I, and all of the others, some of them boys, had been stillborn or had died soon after birth, which must have added to her sadness at the king's rejection of her), and because he was taken with Anne Boleyn. The king's marriage had required a dispensation because Catherine had been married to his brother, who had died, and marriage to a sister-in-law was ordinarily forbidden. The Pope had granted the necessary dispensation, but now King Henry claimed to have scruples about its validity. At the king's request, More studied the matter and saw that the marriage was valid in the circumstances. Henry, for his own purposes, alleged that the Pope had no ability to permit it. More gave his answer to the king but did not make it public.

The Archbishop of Canterbury then declared Henry's and Catherine's marriage invalid, in accordance with the king's wishes, and Henry proposed an Oath of Supremacy tying the bishops to the decrees of the crown instead of those of the papacy. Thomas More was accused of treason because he refused to take this Oath, which assigned to the king the position of Head of the Church, thereby repudiating the position of the Pope as the successor of St. Peter, to whom Christ gave the "keys of the kingdom."[11]

Thomas More was the preeminent man in the land. Many others of less eminence cheerfully, or fearfully, signed the Oath. He was among the few who saw clearly and had the courage to uphold the historic truth of the position of the Vicar of Christ. Even his own family doubted the necessity of his stand, and that must have pained him terribly; because of his great love for his family, it would have been harder to bear than the disapprobation of others. Even his wife visited him in the Tower of London, where he was imprisoned, and said, "I muse what in God's name you mean here fondly [foolishly] to tarry."

From the Tower, Thomas wrote a farewell letter to his daughter Meg, and through her to all his family, his friends, servants, and neighbors, telling them to serve God and "be merry and rejoice in him." He also asked them to pray for him, as he would pray that they "may meet together in heaven where we shall be merry forever."

Thomas More died as a witness to the truth of the authority of St. Peter's successor. It is surely rare in history that a man of such eminence in affairs of state should sacrifice his worldly reputation and even his life for a religious truth.

St. Thomas More was canonized in 1935 and is venerated all over the world, not merely the English-speaking world, as martyr, writer, statesman, husband, and father. He was a great man and a model for both public and private life.

Blessed Elizabeth Canori Mora

"In my Father's house there are many dwelling places," said Jesus.[12] If we take this to mean that very different sorts of human beings will be received in heaven, the contrast between St. Thomas More and Blessed Elizabeth Canori Mora exemplifies it.

She was born in an aristocratic family in Rome in the year 1774 and early in childhood was seen to have a remarkable religious bent. She and her sister were educated with the Augustinian nuns in Umbria, and there Elizabeth deepened her faith and happily "loved to dwell on the things of God." She thought that she might have a vocation to the religious life, but in her teens she developed what was feared to be tuberculosis, and her parents took her home to build up her strength. As she recovered, she was introduced into society and promptly forgot about her possible vocation, coming thoroughly to enjoy social life. She was pretty and dressed elegantly in the fashion of the time; as she said later, "I forgot about God."[13]

At nineteen, she fell in love with a student of law, Christoforo Moro, who was already in love with her. She consulted a priest and decided that her vocation was to the married life. She and Christoforo married and were at first tremendously happy together. He was very proud of her beauty and enjoyed the admiration she provoked at parties and gatherings. However, after some time he became very jealous of her and forbade her to visit her family or friends, wanting to keep her "for himself."

She tried hard and succeeded in being patient, but after some years, he lost interest in her and their children and took a mistress. Christoforo involved himself unwisely in various business deals, which did badly, and he gambled heavily, with the result that his wife and their two daughters found themselves without an income. Elizabeth remained faithful to her marriage in every way, and with understanding and forgiveness she would sell anything she had to keep her husband out of prison for debt and to nurse him when he became ill. It was a lonely time. She brought up her daughters carefully, encouraging them to love their father and to pray for him. Her spiritual life deepened and intensified. She became a lay member of the Trinitarian Order (what is called a member of the Third Order) and worked without care for herself, looking after the poor, the sick, and the prostitutes, while always remaining aware of the love of God for everyone. It may seem strange and unexpected that someone so down-to-earth in her care for those with heavy burdens to bear should also be a mystic, but so she was. She prayed hard for the conversion of her husband and for all sinners at Mass every day and for an hour in front of the Blessed Sacrament. It was the time she spent in prayer that enabled her to continue her work, and she experienced many mystical gifts. Her two children followed her in faith. One of them became a religious sister; the other married but died young, though they both outlived their mother.

After her death, her prayer was answered in an emphatic and remarkable way. Christoforo experienced a profound and lasting change of heart. From being an adulterer and a gambler with a love of doubtful business deals, he became aware of the sorrows he had caused his wife and daughters and his God. His repentance was so real that he was accepted as a friar and then as a priest in the Franciscan Order and lived the rest of his life in great holiness. Elizabeth must have rejoiced in heaven at the change in her husband's heart. She was beatified by Pope John Paul II in 1994.

St. Homobonus

We do not actually know this saint's baptismal name. He seems universally to have been known as "*Homobonus,*" "Goodman." He was a cloth merchant and possibly a tailor who lived in Cremona in the twelfth century. He married, but his marriage was unhappily childless, and so he started to care for children without families or from very poor homes. Homobonus would visit their hovels and arrange for them to receive a good upbringing, supporting them with his own money.

His wife resented his acts of kindness, but he gently helped her to see the importance of what he was doing and succeeded so well that she became his assistant. Homobonus was also much sought after in marriage or family disputes, where his evident holiness assisted in resolving difficulties and bringing peace.

His work was not just enthusiasm for social engineering or do-gooding but sprang from a deep and certain religious faith, which he nourished with daily Mass and praying almost as he breathed. He loved the prayer of the Church and prayed the Office with the priests of the town. He also mortified himself in order to gain the spiritual strength to enable him to help others. He died during Mass (at the Gloria, appropriately enough), aged about sixty-seven. Many miracles are attributed to his intercession. His was an ordinary life, made remarkable by his cooperation with grace. Homobonus was canonized by Pope Innocent III at the very beginning of the thirteenth century. It is such a simple story, yet recognized in the annals of the saints. He offered up his disappointment and sadness that he and his wife had no children in order to give to needy children the sort of upbringing he would have liked to be able to give his own.

We can stretch across the centuries in our imagination and see him, followed by his helping wife, successfully doing by themselves what huge departments of government in our own time struggle to do.

St. Gianna Molla

From times past, we come almost to the present day. Gianna Molla was a thoroughly modern woman. She was a medical doctor who worked all her life, even after her marriage and the birth of her children.[14] She is also a witness to the truth and value of the life of the preborn child in the womb.

Gianna was born in the town of Magenta in northern Italy in 1922, the tenth child in a happy but not wealthy family, and was brought up in Bergamo. Her parents, who were well educated, lived their strong Catholic faith, attending Mass every day (though this meant that her father had to get up at five in order to get to his job in Milan after Mass). The children almost always accompanied their mother to Mass, a little later on in the morning but before school time, although they were not told to do so. In the evening they all ate supper together, and their father would want to know how the day had gone for each of them. If any of the children had been naughty in some way, the parents would frown but say nothing so as not to ruin the atmosphere of the evening. Mealtimes seem to have been noisy, with children and parents discussing all sorts of matters in a lively way.

The impact of Fascism on the life of Italy was increasingly felt, and hate-filled attacks were made on the Church and particularly on Christian Action, the movement for lay Catholics. Mussolini understood the strength of this movement and its power as a barrier to the encroachment of the state, which the dictator wished to be total. He had intended to wipe out the movement completely, as was done by the Nazis in Germany, but finally allowed it to remain as long as its work was confined to the purely spiritual sphere. Catholic Action had been concerned with the formation of the whole person, especially in its work with youth groups, and involved sports, walking and skiing in the mountains, the arts, and so on. Membership in the Fascist youth movement was compulsory but very uninspiring. If anyone refused to join, however, sanctions could be severe. Gianna continued her involvement in the Catholic lay movement, and when the war was over, she was increasingly caught up in it as a student at Milan University and later at Pavia University, where she and her youngest sister both studied medicine. After qualifying as a doctor and surgeon and continuing to study pediatrics, she joined one of her brothers, who was a doctor, in his practice. Her sister Ginia, now also a doctor, had joined a religious missionary Order and was running a medical refuge for lepers in India. One of her brothers, a priest who was a graduate engineer, was working in Brazil. Another brother, also a doctor and priest, was busy in the mission fields.

As a physician, Gianna particularly enjoyed working with mothers and children, but she also looked after old people and the very poor, many of whom had neither private health insurance nor families to assist them. There was no state provision of medical care at that time. Most doctors helped the poor, too, but Gianna went further, even lending money if people were desperate, helping the unemployed to find jobs, and so on. She encouraged women who were unhappy or fearful about a pregnancy, and to any who had terminated a pregnancy she gently explained the reality of abortion, the taking of life in the womb, because a realization of what has been done is essential to healing and repentance.

She fell in love with a man called Pietro Molla who had already singled her out and fallen in love with her after meeting her on a few occasions. She had prayed a great deal to discern her vocation in life and had come to realize that it lay in marriage and family. She was thirty-two when she married, and Pietro was forty-two. She wished, however, to continue her work as a doctor, and he readily agreed.

Her first baby was born safely, after a difficult pregnancy, and she took on a girl to help her in the house and with the baby while she attended to her duties as a local doctor. Savina became part of the family and grew very fond of Gianna, and Gianna knew that her baby was in good hands while she was on her rounds.

Her marriage was very happy; the couple shared many things, including a delight in music—she played the piano—and they often attended concerts in Milan. They also shared a love of the mountains, where they took holidays when they could. Pietro had to travel a lot for his work, and Gianna found being without him difficult. However, she was always busy, and soon two more babies arrived to their great joy.

Gianna then lost two babies through miscarriages; she prayed for another baby and was delighted when one was conceived. Two months into her pregnancy, doctors discovered that she had a fibroma, a tumor in the womb. It was growing rapidly.

Another doctor brother, Nando, and a consultant recommended surgery to save Gianna's life. Gianna agreed to the surgery on the condition that they would make every effort to save the baby. With great heroism, she told them, "If you must decide between me and the child, do not hesitate: choose the child—I insist on it." As a doctor herself, Gianna well knew the danger she was facing.

The doctors had recommended a hysterectomy because of the way the tumor was growing, and of course this would have meant losing the baby. This would have been morally licit since the action was to remove the tumor, not to deliberately kill the baby, which would have been an unintended consequence. (This is known as the principle of the double effect: an action that is good in itself but has both a good and an evil effect can be allowed under certain circumstances.) Gianna's action was heroic because she chose to put her baby's life ahead of her own even though she was not obliged to do that.

After the surgery, Gianna prayed hard for her new baby and for herself, for she loved life and her family and longed to see her children grow up. She also asked her friends to pray. The baby, a girl, was born safely by caesarian section and laid in Gianna's arms as she came round from the anesthetic. Gianna soon realized that something else was happening in her body; she had, in fact, developed septic peritonitis. She suffered great pain but did not want to be made unconscious. It was her brother, one of her two priest-brothers who were also doctors, who gave her the sacrament of the sick. She asked to go home and was brought there, where she died the same morning.

The twentieth century and now the twenty-first century have seen acceptance among many countries and peoples of a throw-away mentality with regard to human life in the womb. Gianna died as a preeminent witness to the reality of preborn life, as real and as valuable as life after birth. The daughter to whom she gave the gift of life at such a price became a doctor like her mother, and with the other surviving children (one had died as a child) and Pietro was present in St. Peter's in Rome in 1994 when Pope John Paul II declared Gianna blessed. The miracle accepted by the Church as being due to her intercession concerned a young Protestant mother in Brazil who was cured when complications developed after the stillbirth of a son. It took place in Gianna's priest-brother's mission hospital in Brazil. Gianna gave everything, more than she needed to give, to witness to and proclaim the sanctity of life in the womb as a gift from God. "Martyr" means "witness." She is a martyr for today.

Gianna was canonized by Pope John Paul II on May 16, 2004.

Franz Jagerstatter

We now travel from one form of martyrdom to another: bravery unto death itself in witness to a man's perception of God's will for the world.

Franz Jagerstatter is not yet a saint, though Ferdinand Holbock includes him in his book titled *Married Saints and Blesseds Through the Ages.*[15] At the time of the Nazi rule in Germany, he was clear-sighted and courageous way beyond the ordinary.

Franz was the illegitimate son of a young country girl in Austria and her boyfriend. They were too poor even to marry, and so in his early years Franz was brought up by his grandmother. Later on, his mother married a farmer, who adopted Franz and gave him his own surname. The family members were conservative, even monarchist, in their thinking, not disposed to support National Socialism, and solid in their faith. In his schooldays he was known as a cheerful lad, but he suffered some discrimination among the other boys at school because of his background, which was well known in the village. When he grew up, he decided to better himself and left to work in the iron-ore industry. There he was influenced by the prevailing socialist ideas of the workforce, which were antagonistic to Christianity, and gave up the practice of religion. However, before long he had to return to his native village because his adoptive father and his grandfather both needed help on the farms.

Once home again, he returned to the Church and began to study and practice the faith with deeper conviction. He started to think of marriage, but in a way that was unlike him, he fathered a child in a relationship that lasted only a short time. The mother of his child said, "We separated in peace. He asked me to forgive him." He regularly provided money for the child's support. It appears that nothing more is known about this episode.[16]

Subsequently, he became engaged to a young woman who deeply shared his faith and prepared with him for marriage in a serious way. He wrote notes on marriage later on when he was in prison, describing each as the "other's self" with the will to "sanctify each other." Franz and Franziska loved each other very much and were happy together. They had three children. They worked hard to farm successfully, and Franz was also sacristan in the church in their village.

Franz clearly understood the evil of Nazism, with its elevation of the state above everything and its hatred of religion, of God, and of the Jewish people. He refused to fight in the war, which he saw as unjust, and was imprisoned because of his conscientious objections. During his imprisonment, he prayed constantly, uniting himself with his family at all times. His wife and children inevitably suffered, but he felt that he had to witness to the faith in that time when such evil was being committed around him and throughout the whole of Europe. In July 1943, he wrote to his family of the future joy of eternity, where they would rejoice eternally "with God and our heavenly mother." He was beheaded in August 1943. His wife, who had had to struggle to accept his brave act and its terrible consequences, brought up their children to live their faith and continued—surely with pride and serenity, and with her children and their families around her—her husband's work as sacristan.

Blessed Luigi Beltrame Quattrocchi and Blessed Maria Corsini Quattrocchi

A most charming photograph appeared in *L'Osservatore Romano* in October 2001. It showed a good-looking, upright elderly gentleman presenting a red rose to a handsome elderly lady with upswept white hair, against a background of mountains. It was a photograph of Blessed Luigi Beltrame Quattrocchi and his wife, Blessed Maria Corsini. Pope John Paul II had long wanted to beatify a husband and wife together, and he was able to do so in the case of these two.

Born in 1880, Luigi was brought up by an uncle and aunt who were childless and had asked his parents if they would permit them to take care of him and bring him up. He kept in contact with his parents and siblings but grew up away from them. He studied law at a university in Rome and became a lawyer, working mostly with banks and in the civil service and in various government organizations of national reconstruction after the Second World War. He had a distinguished career.

Maria was born into an aristocratic family in Florence in 1884 and studied music. As an adult, she wrote articles for various journals on the subject. They had three children, two boys and a girl, without trouble, but Maria's fourth pregnancy was difficult, and her gynecologists suggested an abortion to make sure that she, at least, was saved. She refused, and Luigi entirely agreed with her decision. They feared, suffered, and prayed. Their prayers were answered.[17] The child, a girl, was born safely, and Maria recovered.

The two of them were enabled to make this difficult decision together because of the way in which they had nurtured their faith, growing in Christian love as they attended Mass and received Holy Communion whenever they could. Before marriage, Luigi was an honest and upright man but not strong in faith. His faith grew with hers as they prayed the Rosary together every night and took part in prayer vigils and retreats, and they also deepened their faith by taking graduate courses at the Pontifical Gregorian University.

Their home was a lively place, always open to friends and to requests for help of all kinds. During the Second World War, they sheltered many refugees in their apartment. In happier times, they enjoyed sports and holidays by the sea or in the mountains. Maria worked in many voluntary capacities, including as a volunteer nurse for the Red Cross during the war in Ethiopia, and with Luigi she worked in the apostolate of marriage and family. Cardinal Jose Saraiva Martins, Prefect of the Congregation for the Causes of Saints, said that they "made a true domestic church of their family, which was open to life, to prayer, to the social apostolate, to solidarity with the poor, and to friendship."[18]

Their two sons became priests; one daughter became a religious; and the other looked after her parents in their old age and then looked after one of her priest brothers. Their parents gladly gave their children to God's service. They themselves, as they grew in holiness, decided to make the "most difficult vow of the most perfect," giving up the sexual expression of their deep love for each other, in order to give themselves, in their own way, directly to God. This is a difficult concept for the twenty-first century to accept. We may suppose that it was difficult for them as well; otherwise, their sacrifice would have counted for little. To grow in holiness is ultimately to concentrate more and more on God in a way that the Church herself describes as heroic. As *L'Osservatore Romano* said, "They moved forward with the grace of God on the way of heroic sanctity in ordinary life."[19] They consecrated themselves to God while living their day-to-day life in the world, and this consecration was reflected in their concerns for their family and for others. They were in their forties at this time.

Luigi died in 1951, and Maria lived for another fourteen years, dying in her daughter's arms. In their life together, they shared the joys and difficulties of family life, sanctifying them by placing them in their eternal context as they responded to God's grace.

Marriage and Sanctity

One does not readily think of marriage as a school of sanctity, but these holy men and women, and very many others, reveal marriage as a means of grace *à déux*. Marriage provides a small but fiercely focused light on the struggles inherent in the human condition, which the grace of God and the prayers of the saints help married couples to resolve.

The glossy, magazine view of marriage is false in another way. It presents life as being without suffering or with the certainty that suffering will never occur again. There is perhaps no concept more alien to contemporary life than the understanding that good can come out of suffering. This is, *par excellence,* the Christian view. Our salvation was achieved by the suffering of God's Son on the cross, through which he identified himself totally with us in our humanity. Without suffering, we would never grow as human beings. A toddler suffers bitterly, as we can see from his furious behavior, when he is not allowed to run across the road. He suffers frustration but learns the reality of danger from traffic. An adult may suffer terribly from being unable to get the job he or she wants and learns from his or her personal experience that we have to live through disappointments, however painful.

A parent may want a child to be first in the class and has to learn that children are individuals with their own capacities, which may not resemble those of their parent's dream. We all want to be loved more perfectly than we are; we all have to learn that love is giving rather than receiving. All the saints have suffered in one way or another, and each has come closer to the cross through suffering. They accepted suffering, not in a masochistic way but as a reality through which they would grow in love.

As we saw, a formal establishment of sanctity, a beatification or canonization, requires a great volume of studies and investigations. This is not possible in the lives of many holy married people, so that, if one can put it like this, after the cleansing of purgatory, we can hope to join the millions on millions from times past, whose names we do not yet know, but with whom, please God, we will share the vision of the Divine.

For Further Exploration

1. In what ways do these short histories cast some light on the mystery of holiness in the particular circumstances of married couples?

2. Do you have any favorite saints, especially married ones? How might you put into practice the example of this saint in your own life?

3. What do these stories tell us about marriage?

REFLECTION

Think about saints. Do you find them inspiring or daunting? Do they set impossible standards, or do they tell us about God's mercy? Many people find the teaching of the communion of the saints (the spiritual union in Christ of those who have died in God's friendship and those still here on earth) a great consolation after the death of someone they love. Consider this in the light of your experience.

CHAPTER 10

A Backward Look at
Marriage and Its Meaning

Since the days of the early Church, marriage has been understood as the institution that best safeguards the well-being of a man and a woman and of their children within the loving framework of the two, committed and bonded to each other. Marriage is so much a part of God's plan for the human race that even the pagans understood at least some of its purpose and value, though certain cultures thought nothing of divorce or multiple wives (or, though more rarely, multiple husbands). Judaism developed the idea of marriage and, over many centuries, Christianity considered it and tried to make it known, countering "concupiscence"—that is, selfish desires that turn others (in marriage, "the other") into objects, especially sexual objects, to be used and not respected as equals.

As with all the major teachings of the Church, we have to look into them with some discernment in order to understand them on more than a superficial level. On the surface, and to the secular temper of our times, they sometimes seem to be old-fashioned and inhumane. But when we look again, we see them quite differently. If we take divorce as an example, we may think that if two people no longer want to be together, why should they be held to it and in the Church's eyes remain married forever? But it often happens that it is only one of the two who wishes to leave and get out of the marriage. The other is likely to be deeply troubled and ashamed; he or she is likely to feel him- or herself to be a failure, and this can go very deep. The hopes that they shared when they married, the happy times they enjoyed together, are all negated by marriage breakdown. Where there are children, the evil consequences are multiplied many times over, and the damage may never be completely repaired. As the poet John Donne wrote in his *Devotions,* "No man is an island, entire of itself," by which he meant that everyone's actions for good or ill have an impact on everyone else and on society as a whole. The acceptance of divorce has been a factor in the breakdown of families; it becomes as easy to "catch" divorce as it is to catch a cold. The children of divorced couples are likely to be wary of relationships of their own, even when they grow up, and they may have greater difficulties than others whose parents remained together in upholding their own marriages. They may even fear relationships too much to enter into marriage, even if there is someone whom they really love.

Occasionally, one hears the accusation that the Church really allows divorces, sometimes followed by the words "if the people are rich enough," only they are called "decrees of nullity." A decree of nullity means that a given marriage never existed, in that the conditions for the marriage were not met. One of the couple, perhaps, did not reveal that he or she had already undergone a valid marriage; or one or the other had been pressured into the marriage by a parent or someone else with authority; or again, one or the other may have gone into the marriage without the intention of being faithful to his or her spouse and there were witnesses to this. In such cases, the Tribunal for Marriage used by the diocese will look at the case and give a verdict on it. If the Tribunal decides that there was no marriage, no gift of one to the other, then it will grant a decree of nullity. If there are no restrictions placed on the decree of nullity (and there are no other previous unions of either party to be considered by the Tribunal), then both are free to marry other spouses in the Catholic

Church. (Although in some cases, the Tribunal will place a Monitum [a recommendation] or a Vetitum [a prohibition] upon one or both of the people in the marriage being reviewed. In these cases, the Tribunal wishes to ensure that the factors that made the first marriage invalid are dealt with in counseling before the person is able to be married in the Catholic Church.) To enter a "marriage" knowing that it will not be valid is, of course, a serious sin.

Human beings are not perfect and, in this life, they are not perfectible either, but they can grow in love and improve even up to a ripe old age—though it takes much effort.

This disorder in the human psyche, which we are born with, does not disappear automatically with Baptism—though the guilt of original sin does. The individual has to work through the whole of life to overcome it—but Christ came on earth to restore men and women to the way it was in "the beginning."[1] The beginning, before sin, was the time of integrity in its original sense, oneness without divorce of body and spirit. Christ came to achieve that wholeness of the person by healing the rift within man, both as male and female, through his offering of himself to his Father on the cross. This work of restoration demanded his life, given up for us, and the reality of it is attested by his resurrection from the dead. Our Baptism demands that we follow him in seeking to heal both ourselves and others, especially those with whom we are two in one flesh. This struggle, of course, is not merely the task of married couples but of every individual, whatever the circumstances of one's life; marriage, however, is our context here.

The beginning of real love is a heady time. Everything seems rich and exciting, not as a matter of money but as the richness of the other's reality is little by little uncovered. John Paul II notes that in general, a person is essentially his or her own, an autonomous being. But love changes that, because the person who loves wants to be not himself or herself but the other, and therefore seeks to renounce autonomy in favor of the beloved. John Paul II calls this the "law of *ekstasis,*" whereby a person goes outside himself or herself so as to "find a fuller existence in another"—the real meaning of the word "ecstasy."[2] At its best, this is a slow exploration. Surfboarding the waves of emotion and promise, and a too-quick decision to marry, can lead to subsequent disillusion. For this reason, the Church is wise to demand a period of consideration and instruction before marriage, so that the couple are gently led to consider their proposed marriage at the deepest level. The Church follows Christ in forbidding fornication. He described it as an "evil intention[s]," along with theft, murder, adultery, avarice, malice, deceit, indecency, envy, slander, pride, and folly.[3] Sex outside of marriage is now so widely regarded as legitimate, and even educational, that this prohibition may seem ridiculous. Or perhaps it may be considered as only applying to loveless or casual sex. There were certainly prostitutes living in Palestine at the time of Christ, but there was small likelihood of a young man who lived with his family having sexual relations outside marriage with a girl living in her family home, and young people stayed with their parents until they married. Therefore, Christ could not have been making a distinction between the sort of sexual relationships current today and the use of prostitutes, approving, if tacitly, the former while expressing strong disapprobation of the latter. There would be a difference of culpability, but it is a fact, shocking though it may seem to our society, that the proper name for sexual intercourse between unmarried people, however strong their feelings for each other, is "fornication." It is Christ who tells us that it is one of the "evil intentions" that come "from the human heart."[4]

The Church could not do other than teach what Christ taught, and when one looks at the anxieties of many young and not-so-young people in our own society, one can see the good sense of it. According to statistical studies, many young women in our time decide that they do not want to marry. But as they get older and start to hear the biological clock ticking, they often seem to reverse their view. The Bridget Joneses of this world then start to look with some trepidation for a husband, when their own sexual availability has compromised their likelihood of finding one easily and joining the "smug marrieds." Marriage and family are desired more strongly by women than by men in most cases, despite current fashions in the affluent West. The woman renting or buying her apartment still usually seeks to make it a sort of nest, cozy and as charming as possible, in which to entertain her boyfriend. A young man may do nothing more to his establishment than perhaps stick up a couple of posters and lay in some beer. She instinctively knows her need for stability in order to bring up her children. He may see marriage as an additional burden that he simply does not have to carry, when he has the companionship and more of a girl he loves. He is keeping himself in an adolescent condition, and she often goes along with the arrangement for fear of losing him. Nature has not provided a level playing field in the matter of sexual relations between men and women. If they live together, the lack of commitment in such relationships, as we have seen, weighs heavily and badly on the couple in terms of health and stress, and such relationships founder more easily than married ones, often leaving one of the two badly scarred. If there are children, they are likely to suffer, too.

The work of the restoration of wholeness in body and spirit is a lifelong one for husbands and wives, and their loving takes many forms. The history of salvation shows how difficult it is for human beings to fully live their commitment in marriage. In addition, as Pope John Paul II notes, in ancient times and, one must say, in many later centuries, women who transgressed were judged more harshly than men—even though many of them would have had much less freedom of decision than the men who exploited them.[5] The story of the woman taken in adultery shows Jesus opposing injustice as well as condemning adultery. He says to her, "Go away and don't sin any more."[6]

Even in marriage, the sexual expression of love is an area in which it is possible for one spouse to exploit the other. Holding in mind the "personhood," as Pope John Paul names it, of the other is the remedy for the urge to infidelity, in action or in thought. Otherwise, the mutual gift, the giving and receiving, can be compromised and negated. Yet, after the resurrection of all the faithful at the end of time, our bodies, says John Paul II, "will speak the language of the resurrection," for our bodies are good in themselves.[7]

By then, we will have gone beyond marriage, as Jesus told us when he said, "when they rise from the dead, they neither marry nor are given in marriage, but are like the angels in heaven."[8] When we love God with that intensity, we will surely also love each other, albeit in a different way from earthly love, because we will be glorified beings.

Long before heaven, men and women, as husbands and wives, have to learn to live together. Because the first thrilling excitement of marriage changes, it does not mean that love is diminished. But it does mean that both have to be aware of the other, of his or her sensibilities and concerns, of his or her likes and dislikes, of his or her impatience or patience. They are equal before God, but they are not identical, and their proclivities, though amazingly various, have to be understood as far as possible. When each one ceases to be discomposed or even shocked by the pronouncements of the other, then both can progress to a deeper love, which incorporates acceptance of the foibles of each. "He always thinks he knows best!" "Why doesn't she get to the point more quickly?" "He never really gets things done!" "She is often a bit of a nag!" One can even stop being irritated with the other and start accepting and being amused.

The first child brings with him or her the most earthshattering change in the parents' lives. They will be proud; they will feel utterly grown up; they will feel frightened; and, above all, they will feel tired. Then the red-faced squalling bundle, this gift, who seems entirely wrapped up in himself, will suddenly emerge with a tentative smile at his mother and father and enter into the world of relationships! It heralds that dawn of self-awareness that will lead, in time, to thinking, wanting, loving, laughing, and crying when things go wrong.

This thrilling new relationship is worth enjoying. No one is ever loved as a mother is loved by her new baby, and a little later on the baby loves the father as much. Bringing up a baby will certainly include moments of boredom as well, and parents may long for time for themselves of the sort they enjoyed before the baby's advent. But that is all part and parcel of the experience. In fact, for a mother, it may be even harder to put up with the child during the hours that she spends with him if a caregiver looks after him most of the time. If most of her energies are directed another way, she may come to resent having to spend any time with the child at all. Later on, however, she may come to wish that she had not missed so much of her baby's early years.

When a couple are getting married in the Catholic Church, they are asked to state separately that they intend their marriage to be a loyal and exclusive relationship ordered toward their mutual support and the procreation of children.

Here too, the Church is sometimes seen as obscurantist and rigid. However, whatever our belief or experience of the sexual expression of love, we cannot deny that the most striking, remarkable, far-reaching outcome of the act is the child. Since we believe in a Creator God, the source of all wisdom and understanding, we can see that everything he creates has its own purpose—though, in some cases, such as the proliferation of many species of beetles, we do not understand what it is! The purpose of the sexual act is twofold. It is to bind husband and wife together and to bring children into the world.

The Church has never said that couples should bring into the world as many children as they physically could. Parents have to decide, in the light of their own good and the good of children already born, whether they can bring up another child—though it is unrealistic to "plan" the number of children they want and suppose that everything will pan out in accordance with their wishes. The second, third, or fourth child, or even the first child, may never come. However difficult it is for parents, especially in a consumer society where we expect to get more or less what we want, they will be able, with God's grace—like Homobonus in the twelfth century—to turn their sadness into an instrument and a gift for the good of others. With recent advances in medical science, many couples can be helped to conceive, as a first step by pinpointing the time of ovulation; they can be helped further in ways that are body-friendly and do not involve destroying human beings at the embryo stage (as in IVF procedures). As we have seen, the Creator, in his wisdom, has fashioned women in a way that limits their time of fertility within each cycle. A couple can learn the pattern of the wife's fertility and use that time to conceive and abstain from intercourse at the fertile time (having been properly taught how to observe it) if for a serious reason they feel it is not right for them to have another child at that point.[9]

Yet the Church forbids contraception. How is this different from using the knowledge of the fertile time to avoid a pregnancy? In *Theology of the Body Made Simple,* Fr. Percy puts it very clearly:

> The human body speaks; it has a language of its own. Therefore, sex, a bodily activity, has a language. Sex speaks a language of sensual pleasure; there can be no doubt about this. But it also speaks a spiritual language, a language of love. By touching each other, listening to each other, looking at each other, and entering and receiving each other, a man and woman communicate in the most intimate way. They communicate sensually and spiritually. They communicate as body-persons. Sex speaks forcefully of love.... Contraception contradicts the language of love, the language of the body. It alters the language of love (pp. 49–50).

But, as both Fr. Percy and Christopher West point out, couples are not obliged to have intercourse, and there may well be times when they should not. It might not be easy to abstain, but there are other circumstances—illness, for instance—where it may be necessary to do so. In that case, to abstain shows love, as it does where the couple honestly feel that the time is not right for another child. "Self-mastery," the ability to control one's desires (and not only in the sexual sphere), is the most adult of achievements.

Fertility awareness is working with God's purposes. Contraceptive use is working against God's purposes. West cites a parallel difference between a miscarriage and an abortion. The result is the same—the loss of a baby—but one case was a natural, though very sad, occurrence, whereas the other was intended and deliberately carried out.

Contraceptives of any sort put a barrier between husband and wife, and this barrier can affect their relationship to each other. It is a refusal to make a gift of self. Few couples who use natural fertility awareness, in accordance with their needs, suffer marriage breakdown and divorce. Couples who start to use it often find a fresh closeness and a new affection lighting up their life.

A family of parents and children is a great source of amusement and pleasure. It is not, of course, without its pains. Children can be mulish, sulky, aggressive, and self-absorbed. Parents can be suffocating, careless, and neglectful. Nevertheless, it would be a very dull family indeed who did not relish the back and forth of family life, which includes such taxing moral dilemmas as: "It's my turn on the swing, because he pushed me off"; or the instant perception of advantage: "She's feeling sick, can I have her french fries?" There can also be appeals to sort out an individual's identity: "Isn't anyone going to stop me from being so naughty!"; "I'm sad, can I have a hug?"

There is a parental art in listening to the jokes and enthusiasm of children. There is a rule of restraint in listening to the travel plans, and many other plans, of teenagers. If parents do not sound horrified, the plans may well be modified later. If they do sound horrified, it will be seen as a good reason to propose even more terrifying, high-risk blueprints. Adolescence is the time when it is hardest and most necessary to keep the links going within the family.

Families come into their own when sickness strikes or some other difficult situation arises. Even in this country, where family ties are not on the whole very strong, one hears time and again of children helping their parents, as well as parents lending a hand (and sometimes money) to their offspring. The wider family also provides a constituency of friendship (even if it is interspersed on occasion with anger and withdrawal). Grandparents, uncles, aunts, and cousins to the third degree of kinship all add up to a database of information about the family and its identity and a source of kindly, family feeling. Physical traits that reappear, interests and stories, all help to root us in our place in our world, from which we can grow, develop, and flourish. Relations who did not know of each other's existence seem, according to anecdote, to recognize something in other family members when they meet, which leads us to say that blood is thicker than water.

Trying to live a truly Christian marriage may, at first sight, seem to put a couple right outside the current parameters of society's practice. Yet the married life of Christians often articulates the aspirations of many people, who may think such a marriage too difficult to achieve but nevertheless wish they could achieve it. Very few people, comparatively, set their faces against marriage for their whole life if there is someone of the opposite sex whom they love, and very few have an insouciant attitude to marriage difficulties. One has often heard a divorced person, shaking his or her head in genuine sadness at the breakdown of someone else's marriage, say, "Isn't it sad?" Christian married couples are living the very life that many others envy for its certainty, its strength, its meaning, and its warmth.

There will be times, however, when couples trying to live their marriage as a Christian sacrament may feel isolated. In such circumstances, it is helpful and reassuring to know other Catholic couples, who will share many of your attitudes. If you do not have many Catholic family members or friends, it would be a good idea to make some new friends. Following Sunday Mass, anyone should feel free to talk to anyone else after sharing that sublime experience, and a cup of coffee or tea, which many church halls provide, can make it easy to chat. It is not a question of bombarding people with theological insights or questions, rather a matter of simply getting to know them as fellow parishioners. Some friendships may blossom; others may not.

It is essential for Catholics to attend Mass on Sundays and Holy Days of Obligation to experience the concreteness of the sacrifice of the Mass and to receive Christ in Holy Communion, hidden in the host—a gift more amazing than anything we have ever received! The Church enjoins us to do this, understandably enough. If we claim to love a friend but only want to see him or her once a year or so, our claim appears fraudulent! We do not seem to love that friend very much. To say that we love Jesus while not bothering to be in his presence at Mass on Sundays and Holy Days and actually receive him as food for our souls is to make a hollow claim. We are only giving up one hour in the week, and there is virtue in obeying the laws of the Church, which are formulated for our good. We learn to love the Mass more and more by being there, regularly, as we should.

The Church is amazingly rich in its diversity. There are so many religious Orders: contemplative ones devoted entirely to prayer and active Orders working in so many fields. The Catholic Church must be the greatest individual provider of health care and education worldwide, and numerous other organizations provide spiritual sustenance in the shape of meetings, books, journals, and videos. Helping with parish events or getting other Catholics together to support some particular work of charity that appeals to us is a very good way forward, whether it be collecting clothes for the Society of St. Vincent de Paul, fund-raising for the work of Aid to the Church in Need, or involving ourselves in the projects supported by the Catholic Fund for Overseas Development. Families with young children may feel particularly called to participate in the work of LIFECALL, with its help for mothers in difficulties over a pregnancy. Many organizations offer support and opportunities for prayer and growth for families. Some resources are listed in the appendix of this book. Working in whatever capacity and whenever possible for such organizations cannot help but involve people in many of the big issues of justice and love, and of the hopes and ethos of Catholic families, in the world as it is.

As adults, we need to continue to educate ourselves, however old we are, to deepen our knowledge of the inexhaustible riches of the faith. Reading the Scriptures, alone or with others, reading the lives of the saints, and attending talks or days of recollection all increase our knowledge and love of the Lord. People are usually very busy, especially in the years when their children are small, and it may not be possible for them to attend such occasions at each and every stage in their life. However, times pass, and when children are older, it is a great interest and even joy to look more deeply into Catholic teaching.

For the Catholic, the most important things are those moments of private prayer (with husband or wife, if possible), the Mass, receiving the sacrament of Reconciliation regularly, and receiving our Lord in Holy Communion. Those spouses who come from other Christian traditions are not denying their own beliefs by joining their Catholic spouses in study and prayer.[10]

Prayer is not easy and is only rarely emotionally rewarding. The late Cardinal Hume is reported to have said that prayer was an acquired taste, like beer—though, unlike beer, it is impossible to have too much of it for one's own good. It is not meant to concern itself with emotions, though sometimes the emotions that lead us to pray are very strong indeed. Very few people receive visions, hear heavenly voices, or find themselves levitating, which in any case would be a worry—though some of the saints undoubtedly have done so. Prayer can sometimes seem heavy and blank. Yet on occasion it can light up an individual's universe. Is there anything more touching than hearing a little child saying a prayer? I remember once walking up the hill to the basilica in Assisi and hearing, from a house whose windows were open to the air, the unmistakable voice of a religious sister saying the rosary. She was answered by the voices of old ladies, lulled by the rhythm of the words and the beauty of the images they conjure up, comforted in speaking to their heavenly Mother Mary. That comfort is not a matter of psychological self-deception but a real interchange between heaven and earth.

The Gift

The word that is central to this book is "gift." Men and women receive the gift of life; their love for each other is a gift of God; couples make a gift of themselves, each to the other, when they marry—the man to the woman, the woman to the man—a minor image of the way in which the divine Bridegroom makes a gift of himself completely and continuously to his Bride, the Church—that is, to all of us.[11] The spouses themselves give the gift of life to their children, as co-creators with God, who invites them to this wonderful opportunity and enriches them, as a gift, with the closeness of their loving. The love of their children is a gift to the parents, though the children may not be aware of the gift that they are, and this love can and often does continue until the death of the parents, sometimes intensifying in the latters' old age. Finally, God, who has given us the gift of redemption through his Divine Son, offers us the gift of everlasting happiness with him.

Afterword

I may have written this book, but the ideas and thoughts it contains are almost entirely those of others. It is not an autobiography. And that is just as well. My main sources have been, of course, Holy Scripture, the *Catechism of the Catholic Church,* and the writings of Pope John Paul II, whose unique background in philosophy, theology, and literature, as well as his pastoral experience as priest, bishop, and archbishop in both the communist state in Poland and the secular West, have enabled him, the successor of St. Peter, to think more deeply perhaps than anyone else about marriage, its meaning, and the gift it is.

Writing this book has been a chastening experience, forcing me to look back on my own life as a wife and mother. I have become more vividly aware of how my shortcomings have often been forgiven by my husband and children in remarkable ways. For that, I am deeply grateful to them and above all to Almighty God for the graces and blessings I have received; in the forefront of those blessings stand the gift of my husband and family.

Appendix

Fertility management:

Billings U.S.A.
651–699–8139
Boma-usa.org
Provides instruction in the Billings Method of Natural Family Planning.

Family of the Americas
800–443–3395
Familyplanning.net
Provides instruction in the Ovulation Method of Natural Family Planning.

Institute for Natural Family Planning, Marquette University
414–288–1881
Marquette.edu/nursing/nfp
Provides instruction in the Marquette Model of Natural Family Planning.

Couple to Couple League
800–745–8252
ccli.org
Provides education and teacher training in the Sympto-Thermal Method of Natural Family Planning.

Northwest Family Services
503–215–6377
Nwfs.org
Provides instruction in the Sympto-Thermal Method of Natural Family Planning.

Pope Paul VI Institute for Reproductive Health
402–390–6600
Popepaulvi.com

Provides instruction in the FertilityCare Method of Natural Family Planning and in NaProTechnology.

Diocesan Development Program for NFP
United States Conference of Catholic Bishops
202–541–3070
usccb.org/prolife/issues/nfp

Provides resources on NFP to individuals, teachers of NFP, and diocesan offices.

One More Soul
800–307–7685
Onemoresoul.org

Provides resources on NFP, sexuality, and chastity education.

National Catholic Bioethics Center
215–877–02661
Ncbcenter.org

Provides research, publications, education, and consultations on medical and life issues.

For further resources in your area, you can contact your local Family Life Office

ORGANIZATIONS OF INTEREST TO CATHOLIC COUPLES

Worldwide Marriage Encounter
800–710–WWME
www.wwme.org

Worldwide Marriage Encounter helps couples to strengthen and revitalize their marriages.

Retrouvaille
800–470–2230
www.helpourmarriage.com

A ministry to help couples whose marriages are in difficulty.

Teams of Our Lady
903-535-7864
www.teamsofourlady.org
An international movement of married couples.

United States Conference of Catholic Bishops, Secretariat for
Family, Laity, Women, and Youth
202-541-3000
www.usccb.org/laity/marriage/

National Association of Catholic Family Life Ministers
937-229-3324
www.nacflm.org

Charter of the Rights of the Family

*Presented by the Holy See to all persons, institutions, and authorities concerned
with the mission of the family in today's world, October 22, 1983.*

ARTICLE 1   All persons have the right to the free choice of their
state of life and thus to marry and establish a family or to remain single.

ARTICLE 2   Marriage cannot be contracted except by the free and
full consent of the spouses duly expressed.

ARTICLE 3   The spouses have the inalienable right to found a
family and to decide on the spacing of births and the number of children to be born, taking into full consideration their duties toward themselves, their children already born, the family and society, in a just
hierarchy of values and in accordance with the objective moral order
that excludes recourse to contraception, sterilization and abortion.

ARTICLE 4   Human life must be respected and protected
absolutely from the moment of conception.

ARTICLE 5   Since they have conferred life on their children,
parents have the original, primary and inalienable right to educate
them; hence they must be acknowledged as the first and foremost
educators of their children.

ARTICLE 6   The family has the right to exist and to progress as a
family.

ARTICLE 7   Every family has the right to live freely its own domestic relgious life under the guidance of parents, as well as the right to profess publicly and to propagate the faith, to take part in public worship and in freely chosen programs of religious instruction without suffering discrimination.

ARTICLE 8   The family has the right to exercise its social and political function in the construction of society.

ARTICLE 9   Families have the right to be able to rely on an adequate family policy on the part of public authorities in the juridical, economic, social and fiscal domains, without any discrimination whatsoever.

ARTICLE 10   Families have a right to a social and economic order in which the organization of work permits the members to live together, and does not hinder the unity, well-being, health and the stability of the family, while offering also the possibility of wholesome recreation.

ARTICLE 11   The family has the right to decent housing, fitting for family life and commensurate to the number of the members, in a physical environment that provides the basic services for the life of the family and the community.

ARTICLE 12   The families of migrants have the right to the same protection as that accorded other families.

Notes

Introduction

1. Gen 2:24. All biblical quotations taken from the *New Revised Standard Version* (Catholic edition), unless otherwise stated.

2. Rev 21:9, 2, 3–4.

Chapter 1

1. Rev 21:2.

2. Is 62:5.

3. Published in various FACTSHEETS from Civitas: The Institute for Civil Society, 2005/6.

4. R. G. Rogers, "Marriage, Sex and Mortality," *Journal of Marriage and the Family* 57 (2004), 515–26.

5. B. D. Cox et al. *The Health and Lifestyles Survey: Seven Years On* (Hanover, New Hampshire: Dartmouth Press, 1993); ref. in F. McAllister, ed., *Marital Breakdown and the Health of the Nation,* 2nd ed. (London: One Plus One, 1995), p. 9.

6. Committee for International Cooperation in National Research in Demography.

7. "One Plus One Marriage and Partnership Research," *Daily Telegraph,* 30 December 2002.

8. J. S. Goodwin et al., "The Effect of Marital Status on Stage, Treatment and Survival of Cancer Patients," *Journal of the American Medical Association* 258 (1987): 3125–30, in J. Waite and M. Gallagher, *The Case for Marriage* (New York: Doubleday, 2000), p. 48.

9. In *New Scientist,* December 2002.

10. *Pro-Life Times,* March 2003. The manufacturers were ordered to change the patient information on the packet.

11. Office of National Statistics (ONS), mortality statistics, in *Daily Telegraph,* 23 August 2002.

12. Office of National Statistics, December 2003.

13. M. P. M. Richards and M. Dyson, *Separation, Divorce and the Development of Children: A Review* (London: DHSS, 1982).

14. "Social Exclusion Unit," in *Daily Telegraph,* 29 November 2002.

15. Around the time of the tragic murder of Damilola Taylor in 2001, boys interviewed on radio and TV expressed this view, with a kind of shrugging detachment. But it is hard to know whether this was what they really felt or what they thought would go down well with the interviewer.

16. "Child Development," quoted in *New Scientist,* 17 May 2003, p. 13.

17. It is worth saying that when one spouse dies, the feeling of loss is paramount, but the absence of parental conflict may reduce in some measure the resultant anger and turmoil in the children.

18. Office of National Statistics, *Population Trends 108,* 2002, Tables 3.1–33.3. Also J. Ermisch, "Premarital Cohabitation, Childbearing and the Creation of One-parent Families," ESRC Research Center on Micro-Social Change, Paper nos. 95–17, 1995, from the British Household Panel Study.

19. Office of National Statistics, 2002, quoted in *Catholic Children's Society Newsletter* (Westminster), Spring 2003.

20. He prefaced it with the remark, "I was a baby once."

21. It is often forgotten in this context that it took many hundreds of years for all males to achieve the right to vote.

Chapter 2

1. It is, however, proper for the invitation to come from the bride's parents, unless there are good reasons for not doing so. It again stresses both continuity of families and a recognition of the new situation.

2. Some brides, in line with current fashion, seem to be unaware that it is not the moment for sexual display! Some degree of dignity is required. Too much bare flesh looks out of place.

3. In a nineteenth-century novel set in Ireland, a priest, tongue in cheek, laments the days when a mother just said to her daughter, "Go to confession, and put out your best dress, for you are to be married in the morning!" and the daughter, from being just one in her father's house, became a queen in a little establishment of her own. Canon Sheehan, *My New Curate* (Dublin: Talbot, 1899).

4. The civil laws of each state regarding marriage must be observed, and the couple must meet with the parish priest to make the required preparations before the wedding

5. Mt 16:18.

6. *Catechism of the Catholic Church,* English Edition (Washington, D.C.: United States Catholic Conference, 1994).

7. Ibid., no. 1116.

8. *A Catechism of Christian Doctrine* (London: Catholic Truth Society, 1999), no. 249.

9. God is not, of course, bound by his creation, and can sanctify by other means.

10. Ibid., no. 278.

11. Peter J. Elliott, *What God Has Joined* (New York: Alba House, 1990), xviii.

12. Cf. 2 Cor 5:17.

13. Cf. 1 Cor 6:19.

14. *Ecclesia de Eucharistia,* Introduction.

15. Cf. *Gaudium et Spes,* 48.1.

16. Elliott, *What God Has Joined,* p. 46.

17. Cf. Jn 2; Mt 26:26.

18. Eph 5:32.

19. If the couple went through a civil marriage and now want their marriage to be valid in the eyes of the Church, and if they are free to marry in the eyes of the Church, they can apply for a "convalidation" ceremony in church.

20. In many societies, the choice of spouse was often influenced by the parents, and the young couple assented to that choice. This was probably especially true of girls. Nevertheless, real consent was understood as essential; cf. E. Schillebeeckx, *Marriage: Human Reality and Saving Mystery* (London: Sheed & Ward, 1965), p. 262.

21. There may be slight variations from diocese to diocese.

22. Cf. *The Wedding Service* (Dublin: Redemptorist Publications, 1970).

23. Cf. Mt 19:3–12.

24. Dietrich Bonhoeffer, *Letters from Prison* (London: SCM Press, 1971).

25. Television interview with Martin Bashir.

26. G. K. Chesterton, *Father Brown, Selected Stories* (Oxford: Oxford University Press, 1955), p. 26.

Chapter 3

1. Mt 19:4 and Mk 10:6.

2. Cf. Bonaventure, *Collations on the Six Days of Creation,* trans. Jose de Vinck (Patterson, NJ: St. Anthony's Guild, 1970), XI, 12.

3. Gen 1:1–31.

4. . John Paul II, *Man and Woman He Created Them: A Theology of the Body,* trans. Michael M. Waldstein (Boston: Pauline Books & Media, 2006), pp. 146–50.

5. Gen 2:23. In the Hebrew, there is a pun in the words man/woman, which, I am told, does not translate.

6. John Paul II, *Man and Woman,* p. 160.

7. Ibid., pp. 169–78.

8. Ibid., p. 183.

9. Cf. ibid., pp. 210–3.

10. John Paul II, *Crossing the Threshold of Hope* (London: Jonathan Cape, 1994), p. 228.

11. God says to the serpent, "I will put enmity between you and the woman," Gen 3:15.

12. *Gaudium et Spes,* 24.

13. Cf. *Catechism of the Catholic Church,* no. 1607.

14. John Paul II points out that in Gen 4:1, Adam "knew" his wife, but in Lk 1:34, Mary says she "knows" not man. This is retained in the New Revised Standard Version of the Bible. The Jerusalem translation says Adam had intercourse with his wife and Mary says she is a virgin. "Knowing," I would argue, has a greater depth of meaning.

15. Gen 3:20.

16. Lk 11:27.

17. Gen 4:1.

18. Women too, of course, but it is not their predominant sin.

19. Karol Wojtyla, Pope John Paul II, *Love and Responsibility* (London: Fount, 1981), pp. 22–3.

20. Mt 19; Mk 10.

21. In a parenthesis, Jesus says, "I am not speaking of fornication." This does not mean that he was contradicting himself on a major matter of teaching, just as he was stating it. We may therefore safely assume that it may refer to separation in cases of infidelity, but not remarriage; or it may refer to marriage within decrees of kinship, forbidden by Mosaic Law. In the small communities of the day, such marriages were not uncommon.

22. Mt 19:1–12, 26.

23. This does not mean that there may not be circumstances when a separation between spouses should take place—in the case of serious violence, for instance, or the welfare of the children. Even after legal divorce, marriage remains undissolved because of Christ's teaching.

24. Cf. John Paul II, *Man and Woman,* p. 84.

25. Cf. C. S. Lewis, *The Four Loves* (London: Geoffrey Bles, 1960), passim.

26. This is also true of Judaism and of the Moslem and Hindu faiths.

27. Kenneth Grahame (London: Armada Books, 1988).

28. Beethoven's obsessive love for his nephew led him to pick him up every day from school when he was eighteen years of age!

29. Mt 22:30.

30. Evelyn Waugh (London: Penguin Books, 1986), p. 324.

31. St. Hilary of Poitier, in Patrick Sherry, *Spirit and Beauty* (Oxford: Clarendon, 1992), p. 10.

32. Janet Smith, taped talk, "Contraception: Why Not?" recorded by One More Soul, Dayton, Ohio, 1999.

33. A recent item (2003) in the Catholic press revealed that a couple in France, who admitted they did not ever intend to have children, were bravely forbidden a church wedding by the bishop.

34. E. Schillebeeckx, *Marriage, Human Reality and Saving Mystery* (London: Sheed & Ward, 1960), p. 312.

35. Mt 5:1–12; also in Luke, Mark, and John.

36. The Jerusalem Bible gives "happy," which provides a neat paradox in the case of some of the teachings—"Happy are you when men persecute you...," for instance. "Blessed" in the NRSV translation sounds more spiritual and less secular.

37. Mt 5:27–8.

38. Cf. Jn 8:32. Pornography on the Internet is now seen, more and more clearly, as the gateway to serious and damaging sins.

Chapter 4

1. "Nor spring nor summer beauty has such grace / As I have seen in one autumnal face," John Donne, "Autumnal," *Complete Works,* ed. John Hayward (London: Nonsuch Press, 1946), p. 75. A friend whose husband died young once told me that the most beautiful line in English poetry was to be found in *The Beggar's Opera;* it reads, "Here's to the widow of fifty!"

2. Quoted in Richard D. Gross, *Psychology, The Science of Mind and Behaviour,* 2nd ed. (London: Hodder & Stoughton, 1992), p. 694.

3. Ibid., pp. 693–5.

4. Ibid., pp. 694–5.

5. Jane Austen, *Northanger Abbey* (London: Macmillan, 1934), p. 3.

6. Plato, *Symposium,* trans. Michael Joyce (Princeton, NJ: Princeton University Press, 1961), pp. 544–5.

7. R. B. Burns and C. B. Dobson, *Introducing Psychology* (Lancaster: MTP Press, 1984), p. 528.

8. St. Edith Stein, *Woman* (Washington, D.C.: ICS Publications, 1987), p. 75.

9. This was a development from Judaism, which did at least value the home and placed certain rites and rituals within it.

10. Regine Pernoud, the French historian and archivist, maintains that in the Middle Ages women not only worked in a wide range of jobs (op. cit., passim), but in the Italian states had basic schooling like the boys (p. 63). Pernoud maintains that it was the ideas of Protestantism that inflicted strict limits on women's activity.

11. Ibid., p. 19.

12. Ibid., passim.

13. The fireside itself is now largely a metaphorical concept.

14. This is a piece of original research of my own.

15. Carrie Paechter, in James Tooley, *The Miseducation of Women* (London: Continuum, 2002), p. 36.

16. You will have noticed that this is written by a woman!

17. *Journal of Child Development,* quoted in *Vision for Love,* June 2003.

18. Rom 7:15.

19. Cf. Vatican II, *The Church in the Modern World* (New York: Costello, 1988), 24.

20. Antoine de Saint Exupery, quoted in *Preparation for Marriage* (London: Marriage Care, 1998), p. 1.

21. Hilaire Belloc, "Courtesy," in *Sound of Heaven,* ed. Russell Sparkes (London: St. Paul's, 2001), p. 254.

22. John Paul II, *Mulieris Dignitatem,* 1988, 10.

23. Stein, *Woman,* p. 76.

Chapter 5

1. Janet Smith, "Contraception: Why Not?"

2. Msgr. Angelo Scola, *The Third Hans Urs von Balthasar Lecture,* Catholic Chaplaincy, Oxford University, March 1998.

3. Gen 1:28.

4. Ven. John Henry Newman, *Apologia Pro Vita Sua* (London: Fontana, 1973).

5. See Durex manufacturer's information for users.

6. *Catholic Herald,* 30 January 2004. In 2000, the RCOG accepted an abortion–breast cancer link, on the basis that the work of Professor Joel Brind showed no methodological flaws.

7. Julian Simon, *The Ultimate Resource* (Princeton, NJ: Princeton University Press, 1981).

8. Sigmund Freud. "The Sexual Life of Human Beings."

9. An advertisement seen in a health clinic read, more or less, as follows: "I'm going to a party tonight. Haven't got anything to wear? I wonder if John will be there. Better take a condom in case." It postulates encouraging a silly woman to have intercourse with a man who apparently is not in any way committed to her!

10. Malcolm Potts, *Cambridge Evening News,* 7 February 1973.

11. Regine Pernoud, *Women in the Age of the Cathedrals* (San Francisco: Ignatius Press, 1998), p. 19.

12. *Life Educational Reprint,* 27.

13. Creighton Model information. The charity LIFE uses the same model and gives a figure of 99.6 percent.

14. Report in *Daily Telegraph,* 23 August 2003, citing a High Court judgment in February 2003.

15. Ibid.

16. A young woman, who had just given birth to a baby she felt she could not keep and was going to offer for adoption, once said to me, "I'm glad I've done it this way. I'm glad I've given him his life."

Chapter 6

1. I am not, of course, saying that babies can only be conceived within marriage! But marriage is our context here.

2. In the rare cases of identical twins, they are certainly very much alike.

3. Lk 1:41, Jerusalem Bible.

4. *Evening Standard,* 12 September 2003.

5. Dr. James Le Fanu, *Sunday Telegraph,* 7 September 2003.

6. Parents should never forget that there is in the Western world a positive sea of outgrown but not outworn equipment for babies. Friends, relations, charity shops, and church bazaars are fine sources.

7. Albert Rosenfeld, in *Life before Birth* (New York: Time-Life Education, 1965), p. 19.

8. Lynette Burrows, *Good Children* (Oxford: Family Publications, 1985).

9. Jane Feinmann, *Baby Blues* (London: Ward Locke, 1997), pp. 88ff.

10. Mel Par, in ibid., pp. 94–5.

Chapter 7

1. *Catechism of the Catholic Church,* no. 1655.

2. John Paul II, *Familiaris Consortio* (Boston: Pauline Books & Media, 1981), no. 11.

3. Ibid., no. 18.

4. Mt 19:6, following Genesis.

5. John Paul II, *Familiaris Consortio,* no. 19.

6. Vatican II, *Decree on the Apostolate of the Laity,* no. 11; cf. John Paul II, ibid., no. 21.

7. Gerard Manley Hopkins, "The Bugler's First Communion," *Poems,* 3rd ed. (Oxford: Oxford University Press, 1948). "Housel" = communion, and is also a sort of pun on the word "house"; the tabernacle is like a little house.

8. John Paul II, *Familiaris Consortio,* no. 23..

9. Ibid.

10. "Perfect end" refers to death in the friendship of God—something we would all wish to pray for.

11. *Catechism of the Catholic Church,* no. 1250.

12. Pope John Paul II, 8 January 1989, *The Pope Teaches* (London: Catholic Truth Society).

13. *Catechism of the Catholic Church,* no. 1260.

14. Ibid, no. 1261.

15. As an Irish priest is supposed to have said to his congregation, "It is no use saying you stole a rope and not mentioning that there was a horse at the end of it!"

16. J. Kelly, D. McLeod, and J. Wallace (Oxford: Family Publications, 1990).

17. Christopher West, *Good News about Sex and Marriage* (Ann Arbor, MI: Servant Publications, 2000).

18. Anthony Percy, *Theology of the Body Made Simple* (Boston: Pauline Books & Media, 2006).

19. David Hajduk, *God's Plan for You: Life, Love, Marriage and Sex* (Boston: Pauline Books & Media, 2006).

20. John Paul II, *Man and Woman He Created Them: A Theology of the Body,* trans. Michael M. Waldstein (Boston: Pauline Books & Media, 2006). Also Christopher West, *Theology of the Body Explained* (Boston: Pauline Books & Media, 2003).

21. Gregory Popcak, *Beyond the Birds and the Bees* (Huntington, IN: Our Sunday Visitor, 2001).

22. Alan Train, *Children Behaving Badly* (London: Souvenir Press, 2000), p. 141.

23. Joanna Bogle, *A Book of Feasts and Seasons* (Leominster: Gracewing, 2002) has excellent detailed instructions for celebrating feasts through the year.

24. In some ways, it is easier to make our confession if we go regularly during the year, say once a month.

Chapter 8

1. The Federal Trade Commission has useful information and advice concerning debt counselors and other financial concerns on its Web site (http://www.ftc.gov).

2. Mary Kirk, *The Marriage Work-Out* (Leeds: Marriage Care & Albatross Books, 1996), p. 101.

3. Ibid., p. 87.

4. Ibid., p. 164.

5. Gross, *Psychology,* p. 163. These stratagems are listed in his book.

6. Some people have argued that there is no evidence that people have been directly affected by what they see or hear in advertising or the media. However, recent research on obesity in children shows that they, at any rate,

are directly influenced by advertising—as advertisers have always thought. Are adults so different?

7. Leo Tolstoy, *Anna Karenina,* trans. A. Maude (New York: W. W. Norton, 1995), p. 1.

8. *Gaudium et Spes,* 24.

Chapter 9

1. *Catechism of the Catholic Church,* no. 326.

2. Cf. Dom Bernard Orchard, OSB, *Born to Be King* (London: Ealing Abbey Scriptorium, 1993), pp. 34ff.

3. Lk 2:51.

4. Lk 1:26–38.

5. Gen 1:22–8.

6. Proverbs 31:10–31 gives a picture of the "perfect wife." It is well worth looking up.

7. To be fair, it may be the journalist who invents the descriptions of the god or goddess.

8. In Christopher McOustra, *The More the Merrier,* printed for the Church of St. Thomas More, Seaford, p. 12.

9. In France, even in the thirteenth and fourteenth centuries, girls and small boys were educated in schools together, often in convents, but in cities there were secular schools as well. See Regine Pernoud, *Women in the Age of the Cathedrals* (San Francisco: Ignatius Press, 1998), pp. 60–1.

10. Peter Ackroyd, *The Life of Thomas More* (London: Random House, 1998), p. 143.

11. Mt 16:19.

12. Jn 14:2.

13. Ferdinand Holbock, *Married Saints and Blesseds Through the Centuries,* trans. M. J. Miller (San Francisco: Ignatius Press, 2002), p. 381. An invaluable book on these and many other married saints.

14. Giuliana Pelusshi, *A Woman's Life: Blessed Gianna Berette Molla* (Boston: Pauline Books & Media, 2002).

15. Holbock, *Married Saints,* p. 448.

16. Ibid., p. 451.

17. Why are some prayers answered specifically and others not? How can we know? We believe that no prayer is wasted, even if any one request is not met.

18. *L'Osservatore Romano,* weekly edition, 10 October 2001.

19. Ibid.

Chapter 10

1. Mt 19:8.

2. John Paul II, *Love and Responsibility* (London: Collins, 1982), p. 126.

3. Mk 7:21.

4. Ibid.

5. Cf. John Paul II, *Man and Woman He Created Them,* pp. 271–2.

6. Jn 8:11.

7. Cf. Agneta Sutton in *John Paul the Great,* ed. William Oddie (London: Catholic Herald & CTS, 2003), p. 143.

8. Mk 12:25.

9. See Appendix.

10. Some people question why those of other Christian traditions cannot receive Holy Communion at a Catholic Mass. In fact, they may obtain permission to do so in certain circumstances—as bride or groom at their wedding, for instance, if certain conditions are met, and "by way of exception." The reason that it is not permitted on a regular basis is that Communion demands identity of proclaimed faith. It is the goal of union. See John Paul II, *Ecclesia de Eucharistia,* nos. 30, 43–46.

11. Ibid., no. 48.

About the Author

JOSEPHINE ROBINSON is married with three grown children. She was educated at Oxford, where she studied English Language and Literature. More recently, she was awarded an MA with distinction at the Maryvale Institute of the Open University. She is also the author of *The Inner Goddess: Feminist Theology in the Light of Catholic Teaching,* (Gracewing, 1998) and *Pope John XXIII, The Universal Parish Priest,* (Catholic Truth Society, 2007). She has worked as a volunteer for pro-life causes and for the Association of Catholic Women (England and Wales) of which she is currently chairman.

BOOKS & MEDIA

The Daughters of St. Paul operate book and media centers at the following addresses. Visit, call or write the one nearest you today, or find us on the World Wide Web, www.pauline.org

CALIFORNIA
3908 Sepulveda Blvd, Culver City, CA 90230	310-397-8676
2460 Broadway Street, Redwood City, CA 94063	650-369-4230
5945 Balboa Avenue, San Diego, CA 92111	858-565-9181

FLORIDA
145 S.W. 107th Avenue, Miami, FL 33174	305-559-6715

HAWAII
1143 Bishop Street, Honolulu, HI 96813	808-521-2731
Neighbor Islands call:	866-521-2731

ILLINOIS
172 North Michigan Avenue, Chicago, IL 60601	312-346-4228

LOUISIANA
4403 Veterans Memorial Blvd, Metairie, LA 70006	504-887-7631

MASSACHUSETTS
885 Providence Hwy, Dedham, MA 02026	781-326-5385

MISSOURI
9804 Watson Road, St. Louis, MO 63126	314-965-3512

NEW JERSEY
561 U.S. Route 1, Wick Plaza, Edison, NJ 08817	732-572-1200

NEW YORK
150 East 52nd Street, New York, NY 10022	212-754-1110

PENNSYLVANIA
9171-A Roosevelt Blvd, Philadelphia, PA 19114	215-676-9494

SOUTH CAROLINA
243 King Street, Charleston, SC 29401	843-577-0175

TENNESSEE
4811 Poplar Avenue, Memphis, TN 38117	901-761-2987

TEXAS
114 Main Plaza, San Antonio, TX 78205	210-224-8101

VIRGINIA
1025 King Street, Alexandria, VA 22314	703-549-3806

CANADA
3022 Dufferin Street, Toronto, ON M6B 3T5	416-781-9131

¡También somos su fuente para libros,
videos y música en español!